'Stationmaster here. Your . . . maggots have arrived.'
The voice lost a few decibels for the word 'maggots',
as if somebody else was in the room he did not want to
hear.

'Ah – the maggots,' John exulted. 'We've been waiting for them.'

The stationmaster now spoke with confidence. It
was now confirmed that he had read the smudged
label correctly.

'Excuse my asking, sir, but they are marked
"Urgent" – what's so urgent about maggots?'

'We're starting a wildlife park.'

There was a moment's silence while the British Rail
mind processed the information.

'Starting a bit small, aren't you, sir?'

Peter Spence

Some of Our Best Friends are Animals

Arrow Books

Arrow Books Limited
3 Fitzroy Square, London W1

An imprint of the Hutchinson Publishing Group

London Melbourne Sydney Auckland
Wellington Johannesburg and agencies
throughout the world

First published by Sidgwick & Jackson 1976
Arrow edition 1977
© Peter Spence 1976

Made and printed in Great Britain
by The Anchor Press Ltd
Tiptree, Essex

ISBN 0 09 914780 7

To Jill

Contents

Author's Note

Some years ago, when I was a newspaper reporter, our old news editor used to tell us, 'Behind every door there is a story – go fetch.' He underestimated the yield of some doors, which have behind them not one but several stories, and, in some cases, an endless stream of them. The most fertile door at which I have ever knocked was at Cricket St Thomas in Somerset, through which I first passed as a week-end guest, and eventually as son-in-law to the residents. Seven years earlier this family had bought this thousand-acre estate, and had since turned fifty acres of it into one of the most beautiful and popular wild-life parks in the country. The story of this adventure was not one I had to 'go fetch': I was sitting right on it. I hesitated, piecing it together, feeling that my own fascination was the product of a personal disposition and family involvement. It was difficult to detach myself sufficiently to regard the story as being of wider general interest. After all, there were other wild-life parks, each with its own story, and books had been written about them. Was there anything about this particular park which would justify its own story being written, which would be distinguishable from the rest? I came to the conclusion there was.

Most wild-life parks, or animal collections, have one of three head-start advantages: either they have some stately patronage – a name like Bedford, or a 'home' like Woburn or Longleat; or they have associations with a famous zoological name like Durrell or Scott or Chipperfield; or they have some firm financial footing. 'Cricket – The West

Country Wild Life Park' started out with none of these. It was the brainchild of a farming family who started from scratch and built it up by their own efforts plus 'a little help from their friends'. It flourished against all odds, against all professional advice and expert opinion. Now we can see that the gamble paid off, because that same opinion in its assessment of such parks throughout the country now rates Cricket among the highest. Needless to say, mistakes were made and glaring faults have been exposed, and corrected, which more experienced animal collectors might have avoided. But these in a sense are the essence of this particular story and no attempt has been made to gloss over them.

Taking a leaf out of this family's book, I make no apology for my lack of authority for writing about animals. My scant knowledge of their ways is no greater than that of any countryman or generalist, although I have had the advantage of close observation and access to more detailed information and to the people who know these particular creatures best. I express my gratitude to my informants by naming them in these pages. I am also indebted to Mary Butler who did my typing. The feelings and thoughts I attribute to some of the animals, and the interpretation of their behaviour, are my own – a combination of observation and surmise, which for all I know may be technically at fault. However, a layman's view lies at the heart of this particular story. I cannot, however, be modest about my qualifications for discussing my 'in-laws' – on them, I am unquestionably a redoubtable expert.

PETER SPENCE

I

The White Elephant

For all the sounds of the jungle and the calls of the wild which echo from dawn to dusk across Britain's wild-life parks, there is one noise in particular which can strike terror into the hearts of the people who run them – the front doorbell.

At least this was the experience of John Taylor, who had learnt over the years that the doorbell was one of the most expressive instruments technology had ever devised. He could identify his visitors and the purpose of their call from the way they rang the bell at the door of his park office. A short timid 'ding' would herald someone looking for a home more suitable than a city-centre flat for a python, a parrot, or a monkey. A slightly more confident but perfunctory tone would indicate that a keeper was at the door with news of the imminent birth of a llama, a bulletin on a sick puma, or a request for assistance to get a macaw down from a tree. A long imperious burst would – depending on the time of day – be an irate customer claiming compensation for a camera trampled on by an elephant or for a pair of trousers torn by a sealion. But undoubtedly the most dreaded inter-ruptions of all come with the clamorous and persistent ringing. This denotes a state of emergency, probably an escape. It was one of these urgent alarms which summoned John to the door one summer morning. He opened it upon a group of excited young children.

'Have you lost a sealion?' gasped a breathless little girl.

'I don't know,' said John.

It was not the sort of question he could dodge with a

dismissive 'No, it's not ours – try next door'. But he had grown wary of escape reports, having in the past sent out several futile posses after dogs, cats, cows, foxes, ordinary wild deer and native birds, which had been identified as buffalo, kangaroos, tigers or vultures. What he meant was that if a sealion had been found it was probably one of his, but as to his knowledge no sealion had applied for leave, he was not aware that one was missing. Yet it was more than likely true, since Gert – the sealion – had been out before.

'Where is it?' John asked on his way to the garage to get the ever-ready recapture-kit, ropes and crate, into the back of the Range-Rover.

'Sitting on a car up on the main road,' blurted out one of the youngsters, eager to play an important part in the drama. So Gert was planning a long trip. As the A30, or 'the longest lane in the country' as it used to be called, starts in London and ends at Land's End it would be difficult to pinpoint exactly where she thought she was going, but she had already hitched her lift. One would have thought that Gert's travels from California to Somerset by way of Nuneaton, would have satisfied her wanderlust, but far from being content with the three acres of lakeside woodland she and her two companions, Bert and Daisy, could call their own, she periodically sets off to investigate the unknown, now, it seemed, by any means of transport available.

Visitors who come to the West Country Wild Life Park to see the animals are largely unaware that they themselves are being watched, and their practice of arriving and departing in cars had evidently not escaped Gert's attention. She had obviously associated cars with tourism and come to the inspired conclusion that the motor car must be the key to any bid for freedom. She had climbed on to the roof of a family car as it stopped in a lay-by, and had slipped down on to the bonnet where she waited patiently for the car to drive off, with her nose thrust forward as if this bearing offered a foolproof disguise as a car manufacturer's insignia. She might have got away with it on a bigger car, but this was a Mini and her half-folded body and her rudder slapping at the windscreen like a hysterical wiper obscured the driver's view. He and his family, for whom this was a new experience, had stayed put, but seeing the young witnesses scamper off towards the park, were confident that help was on the way.

Various versions of this situation, in which estimates of Gert's size and the length of her teeth became more and more inflated, were related to John as he drove the children to the scene. There was no sign of Gert or the car. The children swallowed hard and blushed.

'It's eaten it and then burst,' explained a seven-year-old. But youthful shouts from the golf course on the other side of the lay-by hedge revived the chase. Another group of children were chattering in an excited huddle in the rough by a shaded copse. John's party joined them.

'It's a sealion – I heard it roar,' said one child.

'I saw it first,' claimed another proudly.

'Can I have it?'

'No, it's mine. I've been guarding it the longest.'

'Sssshhhhhh – it's asleep,' whispered a considerate little girl.

'So where is it?' asked John breaking through the cordon with his lasso.

'Over there – under that bush.' They all pointed into the copse at a shiny black mound lying in the grass. John approached it cautiously.

'Come on, Gert – time to go home. Gert! Gert?'

He got no response. He was almost on top of it before he realized he was talking to a black polythene bag full of sand. Gert was a little way off, peeping over a bunker and being highly entertained by the absurd goings-on on the other side of the fairway. Eventually she could contain her delight no longer and let out a loud guffaw, giving her position away. Within twenty minutes she was back in her lake, and John, now regarding her as a maximum security risk, had ordered a check-out of her enclosure.

But before any patching up of escape routes could be done, Gert was brazenly planning her next break-out. Drawing on the lessons of her foiled escape, she came to the conclusion that her mistake lay in her choice of car. The little family saloon had not been quick enough on the starting grids, and she reckoned that the car which was going to get her over the hills and far away would have to be something a bit more sporty.

She was in luck. In the lodge by the West Gate of the estate lived a motor-rally enthusiast who owned a natty little M G B–G T equipped with all the trappings of the sport. Working on the theory that another escape attempt would least be expected at a time when the fugitive would be smarting from the humiliation of recapture, Gert took her chance. That afternoon the telltale doorbell rang again.

'One of your sealions is sitting on my car,' reported Chris, the distraught rally driver.

Slinging the crate back into the Range-Rover, John and Chris raced up the drive towards West Lodge.

'It's sitting on the roof. Won't it hurt it?'

'No – she wouldn't sit there if she wasn't comfortable,' said John.

'I mean the paintwork. Won't it hurt my paintwork?'

Gert, from her vantage point on top of the car, saw the Range-Rover approaching, recognizing the danger, and rolled off the roof, on to the bonnet, and slid down the front wing panel to the ground. As she made off up the drive, Chris inspected his car for damage.

'Not a mark on it.'

'Never mind that,' John shouted. 'Get ahead of her and drive her back here.'

It would have been simple for Chris to have walked past Gert and turned her round, yet he succumbed to that human frailty which forbids anything which can be done by car to be done on foot. Perhaps he thought 'drive her back here' meant giving her a lift. After much revving, screeching of tyres, crashing of gears and five-point turns, the little sports car had Gert lolloping back towards the Range-Rover, which joined in this mechanized game of 'sealion in the middle', and eventually snookered Gert's escape.

With the lasso and some hitherto undiscovered wrestling holds, John and Chris heaved 150 lb. of struggling sealion into the crate at the back of the Range-Rover, and the two captors parted. As John drove homewards, the lid suddenly flew off the crate and Gert came leaping over the upholstery and heaved herself into the passenger seat at John's side, causing a landslide of road maps and vehicle maintenance manuals. Sitting with her flippers up on the dashboard, she looked out of the window with an astonished expression on her face like a rally navigator confronted with a roadless mountain range he thought was 200 miles away. There she remained long enough for John to feel confident that it would be safe to drive on. But this involved changing gear from time to time. Gert, however, liked the high gear they were in and every time John put his hand on the gearstick Gert snapped spitefully at his fingers. It was obviously time to stop and put Gert back in her crate. But stopping was none too easy since John could neither change down nor reach the ignition without imperilling his fingers. Gert's mechanical knowledge seemed sufficient to tell her that if she continued to snap, John would have to keep driving indefinitely – if she could not escape on her own, at least she would take her keeper with her.

It was now John who had to plan an escape. If he were to slow down, leave the vehicle in high gear and leap out, the engine would be bound to stall. It was a sound theory which worked in every detail but one. The engine did not stall and John had already jumped out and slammed the door. This was more than Gert could have hoped for. Wriggling over into the empty driver's seat, she rested her flippers on the steering wheel and drove happily down the road, triumphantly honking the hooter. John stood helplessly in the middle of the road as the vehicle moved further and further away showing no signs of stopping.

The M G B drove up behind him.

'Who's that driving the Range-Rover?' Chris asked.

'Oh, it's only the sealion,' said John casually, thankful that the question had not come from a policeman or a psychiatrist. He sprinted after the runaway, caught it up, threw open the door and risked his fingers on the ignition key. Gert was on 'cloud nine' and was not looking. After some more three-handed wrestling Gert was back at the lakeside. Bert and Daisy were waiting on the bank and watched Gert's release with mournful faces, like a Colditz escape committee watching an unsuccessful fugitive being marched back into the compound on his way to the cooler.

'Yaaagghhhh, Yaaagghh,' they chorused. 'Better luck next time.'

The last of the day's visitors were just departing, and a hush descended over the valley when the barking of the sealions had died away. It was time for John's evening inspection of the parklands, the fifty acres of pasture, lakes, woods and scrub which were home to more than a thousand exotic creatures. The deer, the llamas, the flamingoes, pelicans, swans, ducks and cranes were beginning their nightfall regrouping, kind by kind. A barnacle goose was stalking a sika deer, and a few ducks were chasing a rhea. An emu was 'down' – a headless, legless mound of feathers lying untidily in one corner of the enclosure – and had to be checked out. As John approached, head and legs seemed to grow out of the dishevelled heap and the ungainly creature scuttled off towards the lake bisecting a group of jacob sheep. The peccaries had already turned in for the night, and a wallaby was nibbling a slice of brown bread.

John walked the length of the valley, along the tree-lined public thoroughfare, past the rosebeds and shrubberies, and into the walled garden where the caged animals and aviary birds were being fed. A keeper was shunting a trolley laden with trays of fruit between the enclosures, and was talking to another keeper with a broom in one hand and the day's collection of shed porcupine quills in the other. Zanda and Myra – the leopards – had gone indoors for their evening feed. A female Rhesus monkey was nit-picking from the back of her infant, and a well-dined Malabar squirrel was wiping its mouth with its tail. Raccoon, coati and gibbon eyed John cautiously as he made his way towards the aviaries

16

where a vulture stared at him lugubriously, a woodpecker momentarily stopped demolishing its cage frame, and a mynah bird called 'Goodbye'. A peacock strutted out of a tulip bed on to the path in front of him and took off to alight clumsily on the low wall of the otter's holt. A civet cat – anxious not to be missed in the food round – was pacing its compound laying a scent around the perimeter with its tail. Until recently, John had usually been accompanied on this tour by a leopard cub on a lead, whose presence was acknowledged by a hubbub of danger signals being transmitted from cage to cage. Before that, his companion had been a young camel which needed exercise, and which set the dingoes howling, the gibbons hooting and the elephants trumpeting. But everything seemed much quieter these summer evenings. The dominant sounds were his own footsteps, the shrill song of the whistling thrush, the muffled 'boom' of the crown pigeon, punctuated by an intermittent snore from a raccoon, the odd whimper from a puma, and the occasional thwack of a branch springing back as a lynx leapt to a better observation point in its well-vegetated pen.

It was late in the evening before John was back in the park office, where the day's paperwork, which might have been dealt with had not Gert decided to sabotage the routine, was still piled up on his desk. Sitting on top of the in-tray was a letter addressed to the managers, the West Country Wild Life Park, Cricket St Thomas, Somerset.

Dear Sirs,
I would like you to know how much we enjoyed your wonderful wild-life park last week. It is indeed a little bit of heaven. Surely Paradise could not be more beautiful.
Yours faithfully,
E. K. Robinson (Mrs)

This was praise indeed. Ten years of appreciative correspondence had not produced such an accolade, but perhaps Mrs Robinson was being too generous. Certainly what he had just seen of twilight in the valley had a heavenly quality about it, but Gert's misdemeanours, which had taken up most of the day, smacked more of the other place. Paradise, John mused, might be a very pleasant place to go, but it could not be a very easy establishment to run. He contented himself with the thought that even if life in the park was at times trying it had at least borne fruit in enriching Mrs Robinson's. It was a satisfying reflection which made all the last ten years of building up a wild-life park from scratch seem worthwhile. A story came to mind – culled from his father's inexhausible repertoire of old jokes – about a vicar walking in a magnificent garden, and saying to the gardener, 'Isn't it amazing what you and the Lord have done between you?' 'Ah yes,' says the gardener, 'but you should have seen it when the Lord had it to himself.' Strictly speaking, the Lord had never had the Cricket Estate to himself, but he certainly never intended it as a wild-life park, nor did he envisage it competing with paradise. John sat back in his swivel chair, and cast his mind back to the time his family had first arrived at Cricket ten years before. The office, with its filing cabinets, overflowing in-trays, cash boxes, estate maps, animal pictures, enclosure designs, feeding schedules, and its pile of lost-property crested by a tartan cap, reverted in his imagination to what it had originally been – a butler's pantry. The silver safe in the far wall was still there, and so were the old glass-fronted crockery cabinets, but gone were the sink, which had once stood where he was now sitting, and the old electric cooker which used to be just inside the door. He remembered that cooker because many a cook had been bowled into the oven if the door opened while she was bending down to examine a joint. It was in this room that his family had met just after they bought the estate. It was mid-winter and the rain was bucketing down outside; there were no curtains on the windows, no hot water, no heat nor light, and there was nowhere to sit. The previous owners had left and the new ones were standing huddled in their overcoats surveying the bare shell of their new property – John, and his father and mother, Paddy and Doreen. It was a gloomy meeting.

18

After a long silence, which only accentuated their physical discomfort, Paddy spoke.

'Well, what are we going to do with the place?'

It was a question they could have done without at that moment, but one which had to be asked sooner or later. 'The place' was a fifty-roomed mansion with seven bathrooms, three kitchens, a ballroom, billiards room and library, and a central hall – an old courtyard – big enough to park eight double-decker buses round the staircase balustrades, and corridors enough of it to run several bus services. Apart from the odd deer – or moose – head peering at them from their wall mountings, a billiards table, and a carpet or two and a few oddments John had brought with him, there were no furnishings in the place. The job-lot they had bought also included sixteen acres of gardens, more than a thousand acres of pastures, arable land and lakes, four farms, seventeen cottages, assorted herds and flocks of livestock and agricultural buildings and equipment – and it had set them back a cool quarter of a million pounds.

What made the prospects so daunting was that they did not have a quarter of a million pounds. The previous few weeks had been spent raising money and even when every financial resource had been sapped they were still far short. They could draw little financial comfort from the fact that the house itself had been designed by Sir John Soane who also designed the Bank of England – even that was short of funds at the time. But they were committed to buying. The previous owner wanted to sell up quickly, and a quick buy was the only way of securing the place at what seemed a remarkably reasonable price. All their efforts so far had brought them to square one – 'ownership' – but, as in many games of chance when the players are at square one, someone has to throw a six to move off, and this particular dice seemed loaded against them.

Yet there was an element of good sense in what the family had done. John had hitherto been a land agent in Suffolk, and wanted to farm. Paddy was already a farmer of some twenty-five years' experience, and both realized that to farm successfully in the current economic climate they had to think in terms of large acreages. Between them they could manage the thousand acres of farmlands; a combination of youthful energy and experienced guidance made them approach that aspect of their future with a measure of confidence. The estate had many attractive features. For one thing it offered magnificent shooting, which endeared it to Paddy, a devotee of the sport. It also had all the signs of being self-sufficient; it had its own forge, workshops, sawmills, builder's yard and even its own glassworks, all fully equipped and complete with a blacksmith, carpenter, plumber, painter and mechanic to go with them. The estate also pumped its own water, and had its own church, complete with vicar and gravedigger, and schoolroom. One could live, work and die without having to leave the estate. But besides all this the estate was beautiful, undeniably one of the loveliest valleys in England. Any right-minded person would have liked, if not to own it, to see it preserved and to spend time there. To own it would be too much of a pipe-dream, even for John, who had no reason to think when he first became acquainted with the place that it one day might be his – and certainly not within a matter of months. Had it not been for a curious sequence of events in which fate played a prominent part his pipe-dream would never have materialised.

Professional routine had first brought Cricket to his attention, when as a land agent he happened to be thumbing through a copy of *Country Life*. The illustrated page advertising the sale of the estate did not interest him particularly as it was like so many others in the same journal. A fleeting thought that it might be agreeable to own a place like that soon gave way to more mundane preoccupations – chief among them being the sale of his car. It was when these two unrelated thoughts – the sale of the estate and the sale of the car – came together that the egg of the Cricket adventure was fertilized. The car was a Triumph on the threshold of mechanical menopause and ripe for a change of ownership. John had found a buyer in Exeter prepared to pay a hundred pounds more for it than anything he had been offered in Suffolk, and this made a trip down the A30 to deliver the vehicle a sound investment. That trip would take him right past the Cricket Estate, and a short detour would enable him to see 'in the flesh' what he had seen in print that morning.

The following evening, on the eve of their first wedding anniversary, John and his wife Rosemary were taking that detour. A boisterous gale was blowing as they turned off the main road and drove down a gullet of trees into the valley. The dark avenue of beeches seemed to swallow them up and the headlights played on the branches to make threatening shapes like little demons darting off into the bushes. Eventually the trees were behind them and the headlights picked out the house, which, silhouetted against the twilight sky, seemed to lean forward to engulf them. It was a spine-chilling sight – everything Hammer Films could have wished for, a mixture of Baskerville Hall and The Grange and all the other spooky mansions where hunchbacks answer creaky doors and beckon you through the cobwebs to the Master's laboratory. Unlike the young intrepid couples in the films, John and Rosemary lost both courage and curiosity and fled back up the drive to the main road, never wanting to return. Yet something made them. Perhaps it was the new car, which so often is capable of rekindling the fire in the belly of the young to give them the confidence to take the whole world on, but the following afternoon a new Triumph hurtled down that drive on its way back to Suffolk. What John and Rosemary then saw before they approached the tunnel of trees was a magnificent heart-stirring sight. The whole valley was spread out before them, the house nestling in the trough with its windows glinting in the sun, surrounded by vast lawns rolling down to lakes banked by woodland pastures stretching as far as the eye could see. This was Cricket St Thomas in its full splendour. It was love at second sight. They made up their minds there and then that this was where they were going to live.

Four months later, when that same vista was a carpet of snow, it was a rickety old van which came thundering down the drive – its open rear doors strung together across protuding bed legs, ladders, tallboys, and umbrella stands. On the roof, surrounded by tea-chests and trunks, two black East Indian ducks were nestling in a basket, quacking indignantly as the vehicle took the bends, as they had done round every corner for the last three hundred miles. Thus, Suffolk and the old life behind them, John and Rosemary arrived to embark on their new adventure as the Squire of Cricket and his Lady, and the ducks as the first incumbents of an as yet unthought-of wild-life park. That vanload of chattels made little impression on the fifty-roomed mansion, just as the ducks were hard put to it to justify the three acres of lakes which were their new home.

For their owners, home was to be one room. Selecting a first-floor bedroom commanding a western view of the valley, there they camped, sleeping on a mattress on the floor. They had slipped in almost unnoticed, although their presence was known, and there had been much speculation on the estate about the 'new people'. Many of the estate staff called at the 'Big House' the following day to offer all kinds of assistance as John and Rosemary busied themselves with household arrangements, and were able to have their anxieties about the new owners confirmed or allayed. The new arrivals were too preoccupied with the finer points of settling in to be daunted or even aware of the awesome dimensions of the monster they had taken on. For John the only hint of it came with the nagging thought that the interest on the place alone was costing him £60 a day. For Rosemary it was the long walk to the lakes to feed the ducks, some thirty times the distance of their old Suffolk duckpond. Their first formal public appearance was at church the first Sunday morning. The service was attended by a sparse congregation of which the most prominent figure was a lady who had owned the estate several months before and now lived at the Dower House. She sat in the family pew with her dog, an adenoidal Pyrenean mountain dog, which snored through the sermon. Her pew was in one of the transepts set at right angles to the nave and chancel, so that much of the service had to be intoned round the corner for her benefit. The memorial plaques round the walls also caught John's attention. The names of the dead inscribed in brass and marble all seemed to have a distinctly naval ring about them – Alexander Hood, Horatio Nelson Hood (two of them), Horatio Nelson Bridport, William Earl Nelson, William Nelson Hood. What would they all be about?

John was officially inaugurated as the new governor at a get-together of the whole estate in the old manor school-room that evening, over coffee and doughnuts. There was Henry, Bill, Ron, Archie, Alan, Jan . . . the names kept going round in his head and coming out to the wrong person in conversation. As they met each one he and Rose-mary were aware of the same thought going through every mind. Perhaps they had expected the new boss to be a moustached army colonel, just retired, or a business tycoon wanting a change of air, or a seasoned farmer come into some money. Instead they were getting a fresh-faced twenty-three-year-old, and his fledgling wife of twenty-one. One after another the men bearded John, soliciting his attention for this or that pet project or requesting a piece of equipment, each suggestion thrown out as a huge joke but meant in deadly earnest.

'I would have dressed up for this do,' said the game-keeper, 'only my suit's worn out and I'm just due for a new one.' John knew that one suit a year on the estate would probably go with the job, which meant he would have to pay for it. The remark was typical of the strategy by which new tractor parts, a replacement sheepdog, a stock of fish for the lakes, new lambing equipment, new ploughs, and new release pens were requisitioned.

'And I forgot to ask him for a new winch,' John heard Henry the tractor driver, saying as he left the party. He now began to realize how much there was to be done, and to understand that what constituted a big job was a conglomeration of little ones. His notebook was full before he had set himself to any single task. He had wanted to develop the farming, but it looked as if keeping the present operation going might take up all his time, particularly as he had his own domestic arrangements to sort out and still had so much more money to raise before the whole deal could be clinched. But on top of these anxieties came a devastating and unforeseeable bolt from the blue. That night Rosemary, six months' pregnant with her first child, developed the first symptoms of encephalitis and was rushed into hospital.

Encephalitis is a virus infection of the brain and for Rosemary – sometimes in a coma, sometimes delirious – the battle against it was a life and death struggle for both herself and the child. The worries of the estate now seemed insignificant in comparison. The situation was to some extent eased by the arrival of Paddy and Doreen. By now they, too, had put all their resources into the venture, left their midlands farm, and embarked on their new life in Somerset, not even sure at this stage where they were going to live. But finding themselves in an empty fifty-bedroomed house, this was the least of their worries.

It was against this backdrop of circumstances that the parley in the butler's pantry took place. Paddy's £250 000 question 'What shall we do with the place?' was a projection into the distant future. He knew that farming alone would not provide enough money to pay off the mortgage interest, nor the capital needed for essential development. He also knew that the estate could only be profitable if the farming was combined with some other enterprise. But what? Answer came there none. The meeting was interrupted by the arrival of two pantechnicons bearing their furniture – the accumulation of twenty-five years of marriage and its five children – as opposed to John and Rosemary's year's worth which only needed a small van and a roof-rack. There was a few days' work just sorting that lot out which Doreen supervised, placing sofas and armchairs in stategic positions and opening up gate-legged tables to make the vast rooms look full. Some rooms had just been decorated, but others, the better-placed living rooms, had been gutted and stripped and the work abandoned when the previous owner decided to sell. They rejected a thousand-pound tender for the job to be finished professionally and decided to do it themselves: a month's work. On the farms there would be several weeks' work scaling the over-subscribed operations down to manageable proportions and changing over to more profitable lines. Everybody's lives were to become diversified and full, particularly John's, whose days were spent installing milking parlours, evenings at Rosemary's hospital bedside and nights helping the shepherd lambing that spring's four hundred ewes. There was not much time to consider embarking on a sideline, but it was becoming more and more urgent.

The idea for a wild-life park did not arise for some time, although the nature of their present situation might have suggested it. They had bought a white elephant. The expression 'white elephant' originated in Siam where an ancient king used to present white elephants to courtiers he wished to ruin, hence it has come to describe any possession the expense or responsibility of which is more than it is worth. This seemed a fair description of Cricket. But the Taylors developed a suitably buoyant and indestructible psychology built on a determination that this particular white elephant was not going to ruin them but was going to work for them. Yet they could not proceed with the job with anything approaching the required amount of zeal while still hampered by financial insecurity. The only way round this was to find outside investment. They put an advertisement in *The Times* which was seen in London by a retired Somerset Light Infantry major, with both money to invest and a desire to do something enterprising in his retirement. Within a matter of weeks Major Jasper Ogilvie had joined the partnership and was living on the estate so as to take an active part in the venture. His arrival solved the immediate financial problems, but it also clarified the family's domestic future. Major Ogilvie had installed himself and his family in the Old Parsonage, the second largest house on the estate, where the senior Taylors might have lived, if the 'big house' was ever put to some commercial purpose. But now the two Taylor generations would have to stay where they were and share Cricket House. Two new arrivals soon justified their occupation of such a vast mansion.

The first was the arrival of Grandma – Paddy's eighty-six-year-old mother – whose move to Somerset severed the family's connection with the midlands for good and all. She was delivered by car at the same time as the local hunt was meeting at the house and the forecourt was aswarm with horse-boxes, hounds, horses and huntsmen knocking back their stirrup cups proffered by Doreen from a silver salver.

'You shouldn't have gone to all this trouble, dear,' said the old lady as she marched into the house through the mounted guard of honour. The other arrival occurred at the other end of the generation spectrum. On 17 June 1966 infant cries issued from the main bedroom of 'Mrs John's half', when Celia was born – it was the first birth in the house for almost exactly a hundred years. In spite of Rosemary's illness from which she had not yet fully recovered, both mother and child were doing well. There was no looking back now. The birth of a child always turns the thoughts of a family toward the future and solidifies its commitment to the present. Doreen had an apt saying at her disposal for every occassion. For this one it was:

'There's never a baby born without a loaf of bread in its hand, I always say.'

'Yes, you always do,' said Paddy.

After all, they had had *five*.

A new chapter in the family history had begun. Soon the house was looking like a home. The Taylors began to like living there, as soon as they got used to its formidable size. The vast distances between rooms were in one sense inconvenient, but they kept the family fit. John calculated at the end of one day running about the house that he had walked fourteen miles, and for the first few weeks there was not a pair of legs in the house which did not ache from over-exertion. Considerable activity in one side of the house would often go unnoticed by people working in another. The domestic arrangements would sometimes go awry. Rosemary would cook a meal in one kitchen which she Paddy and John would eat in the dining room, whereupon Doreen would bring in another meal which she had been cooking in another kitchen. But whatever anybody was doing in the house, the family always viewed it with an ulterior motive. How could it be used so that it paid for its own upkeep? Various ideas were constantly under discussion.

'What about a health farm?' suggested Paddy one morning as he counted an even number of grapefruit segments – a sure sign of a good day ahead. 'We could turn the place into a health farm for businessmen . . .'

'. . . Only instead of diets, isometric wheels, and bikes and rowing boats which don't go anywhere, we could have them working on the farm mucking out and humping bales,' continued John. While Paddy liked the idea of a labour force actually paying to work for him, he was sceptical. After all, twenty-five years of heavy farm work had not done much for his own waistline. He was now up a ladder in the hall putting a new eye into one of the stuffed moose-heads.

'What about Americans? If we had Americans staying here we could give them a typical British weekend in a stately home; they could do hunting one day, shooting the next, and we could lay on a ball and a banquet in the evenings.'

'Maypole dancing, falconry, jousting,' John went on.

'You'll want to do bear-baiting next,' Doreen protested.

'Well, we've got a licence for it – look.' Paddy was unhooking an ancient document from the wall. It was an ornately scripted parchment dated 1467, bearing the Royal Seal of King Edward IV – empowering the Lord of the Manor of Cricket St Thomas to hold fairs on his estate.

'That's us,' Paddy deduced. It was a humble claim, since this family's station in life – that of yeoman's stock – was far more lowly than most of the previous lords of the manor.

'It's a pity that Horatio Nelson never actually lived here,' John said, knowing that he could be doing a good tourist trade if he had. In fact, Horatio Nelson appeared to be about the only great naval figure who had not lived at Cricket at some time or other, although the legend had it that he was a frequent visitor. Bridports, Hoods and Rodneys established the estate's tradition of naval patronage. Another owner had been Sir Amyas Preston, a hero of the British fleet at the time of the Spanish Armada. In 1757 Cricket had become the home of Alexander Hood, whose distinguished naval career earned him the title Baron Bridport. His brother Samuel was also an admiral and had commanded a Mediterranean fleet in which served a young captain who later, it is believed, commanded his great-nephew at the Battle of the Niye. That captain who served under the one Hood and commanded the other was Horatio Nelson himself. The two families became related by the marriage of Nelson's niece, Charlotte, to Samuel – Second Baron Bridport – and they lived at Cricket, but this marriage was five years after Trafalgar. Although Nelson was by then dead, it is thought that the two families were friends long before this marriage, in which case it is quite possible that Horatio himself visited Cricket long before he became a national hero. Certainly the Bridports were persistent in their efforts to keep his name alive by giving it to a series of short-lived sons, whose memorials adorn the walls of Cricket church.

'I'd like to think he came here often,' sighed Doreen, the antiquarian of the family, 'but I don't think he did.'

Paddy objected, 'We can't tell Americans that. After all, there's all that Nelson stuff in the church, there's the cedar tree, and there's Admiral's Seat.'

The cedar tree, which stands not far from the house, was thought to be a trysting place where Nelson and Emma Hamilton may have dallied, but no ensigned trouser button has been found there to prove it. 'Admiral's Seat' is an un-prepossessing stone summerhouse set in a hill about half a mile from the house. Had Sir Christopher Wren ever been asked to design a bus shelter this would have been the result. It had once stood on top of the hill, but had since been rebuilt in woodlands further down; by all accounts the original loftier position gave 'The Admiral' a clear view of the fleet anchored at Lyme Regis. The identity of the admiral after whom the edifice was named remains a mystery. It might have been Nelson himself, but as that hill has in its time been scaled by several resident admirals and their friends, presumably other admirals, it could have been made after any one of a number of old salts, or even all of them.

'We just don't know,' said Doreen, who had been at pains to explain the full range of possibilities. 'I've read six biographies of Nelson and not one of them mentions any visit to Cricket.'

'And I bet there wasn't any mention of his going to the lavatory, but that doesn't mean he never did,' Paddy declared defiantly. 'I'd like to be able to give these Americans the full Nelson works.'

With that he went into one of his performances. Paddy's acting routines could always be relied on to put his audience in cheerful spirits, and were a godsend to the family in difficult times. He had an endless supply of old gags, but he never told them as jokes, instead working them into his patter so that nobody recognized the story until he was into the punchline. Thus the most familiar jokes could be recycled so that he never had to learn new ones. He was also an impish prankster. He would introduce two people at cocktail parties, having briefed each beforehand that the other was deaf, and then leave them bellowing at each other in a corner. One evening, surveying the great hall at Cricket, the family thought that the alcoves needed filling up with Greek statues. That night on their way to bed they found their prayers had been answered. Paddy had stripped off and was posing in one of the illuminated recesses with a bowl of fruit on his head. But now John, Doreen and Rosemary were in for a Nelson routine. Paddy was doing a stately-home guide.

'As you come in through the main door you see the main hall, which has been preserved just as it was when Nelson first visited the house. You all know about Nelson: the hero of Trafalgar whose eye fell out and knocked his arm off. And here you see the billiard table where he used to play snooker in the late winter evenings, while waiting for Lady Hamilton to come out of her boudoir. On the cues here you can see the marks of the Admiral's braid sleeve bands on the handles, and here you can see where he ripped the cloth.' (In fact he and John had done that, an accident he was prepared to overlook for the sake of historical perspective.)

Paddy now led his party into the dining room and took up a position by the sideboard.

'Gather round, ladies and gentlemen. Now here you see a scratch on the front panel, and this Nelson did with the pin he used for keeping his loose sleeve out of the gravy. And this . . .' he picked up the electric toaster, 'I must be honest about this. The experts don't think the Admiral used this an awful lot.'

There was no doubt that the spacious rooms and the guide's voice echoing through the halls created the right atmosphere for conducted tours of this kind. It seemed a pity that the supply of exhibits and authentic historical material was lacking. They could not bring themselves to dishonour Nelson's treasured memory, nor distort and inflate the facts on such slender evidence, for the sake of a fast buck, even though some of them might be true.

Other ideas for turning the place into a restaurant, a hotel, a banqueting hall, a conference centre, and even flats, flew around freely. One notion which ranked quite highly in the scale of possibilities was that half the house should be a stately home for stately old folk, offering first-rate private nursing. John liked the idea, but Paddy and Doreen were against it, uneasy about which side of the house they might ultimately be billeted. Besides, they had a better idea. Why could they not open the gardens to the public?

It was their first spring at Cricket, and they were only just beginning to see quite how magnificent the gardens could be; after all, they had never seen them in summer. Daffodils and crocuses adorned the banks, and over the sixteen acres of garden, trees and plants were beginning to blossom, bud, and bloom. These were no ordinary gardens. Years earlier one of the Bridports had been a dedicated horticulturist, and had been meticulous in landscaping and cultivation. Some say that he overspent himself on the gardens, which was why that family eventually had to sell up. He had imported a multitude of rare trees and plants, and his enthusiasm was shared by subsequent owners up to the turn of the century. The estate now bristled with cedar, bamboo, Cryotomeria, Gingko Bycloba, Sequoiaden-dron and monkey puzzle and the over-all effect was of a beautifully unified design, composed of contrasting colours and shapes. By summer the rosebeds, the rockeries, the herbaceous borders, and shrubberies would present a dazzling profusion of colour. No one family would be entitled to such beauty, not this family at any rate. Opening the gardens for all to see was almost a foregone conclusion. Besides, maintaining them was already consuming much of the family's spare time, and even weekend guests who said that they would like to spend the afternoon sitting in the sun found themselves doing so on the roller-seat hitched to the back of the motor mower.

It was while all hands were employed with fork and trowel, and the show gardens were taking shape, that the seeds of an even better idea were sown. The thought loomed out of the pages of *The Sunday Times*. John had caught sight of an advertisement during lunch, a meal which sometimes subsides into long periods of silence on a working day, due to a long-standing family injunction which forbids the menfolk to discuss farming at table.

He broke the silence and read aloud:

31

'Make your garden pay. Do you have a stately home or large estate and need management advice? Consult Associated Pleasure Parks, Yorkshire.'

'Associated Pleasure Parks. Who are they?' asked Doreen.

'I think they run a wild-life park somewhere,' Paddy recalled from his reading of the business news.

'A wild-life park? Mmmmm,' John murmured thoughtfully.

'A wild-life park,' echoed Paddy. A moment's silence honouring the angel passing overhead was broken by Doreen.

'Anyone want a banana?'

2

The Great Afterthought

'Three lions arriving first thing in the morning,' John announced casually, wandering into Rosemary's kitchen. It was the first Rosemary had heard of the wild-life park idea.

'Now that I like,' she said enthusiastically. She had got used to John coming up with hare-brained notions and knew instinctively what his emphatic statements meant. She had heard some pretty wild ideas over the last few weeks, but this sounded sensible. To John nothing was just 'a thought' or 'a possibility', it was a fact. It would have been uncharacteristic for him to have begun at the beginning and said, 'We're thinking of starting a wild-life park.' Rosemary knew that the bit about the three lions was invented for effect.

'Yes, I really like that idea,' she agreed when John had toned down his account of what was envisaged. What was so surprising about the idea was that nobody had thought of it before. It was an afterthought which for months had been smothered by a succession of more obscure ideas, but which had all along been staring them in the face. The view along the valley with its line of lakes was spectacular. Moreover, as it was not suitable for farming, it was natural for such a venture – and it did not require any great stretch of the imagination to visualize wild deer grazing on the slopes, and flamingoes, pelicans, and wild duck living on the lakes. Already the idea of opening the gardens to the public had been proved plausible, and to make the adjoining valley a sanctuary for exotic creatures to add to their attraction seemed the next logical step.

John wasted no time in contacting Associated Pleasure Parks, and discovered that their advertisement was offering more than management advice. The company was offering the wherewithal to set up a wild-life park, expert know-how, people to run it, and, best of all, the animals themselves which would come from Flamingo Park in Yorkshire. One visit was enough to convince their management that Cricket was ideal. For all John and Paddy knew, the only thing the valley needed was one ring fence, and the animals could be let loose into it. They were wildly wrong, and soon found that animals required much more sophisticated development. But now the future of the estate suddenly looked more promising. The estate itself started to look different. Children's puzzle books often feature outline drawings of an empty jungle with a caption underneath saying, 'How many monkeys can you find in this picture?' You then scrutinize the drawings closely, whereupon monkeys' faces appear in the rings of fallen trees, in the twists of the branches, in the whorls of the leaves, the ripples of the waterhole and the contours of the distant mountains. This was how everybody began to look at the estate, seeing imaginary baboons, crocodiles, snakes and elephants emerging from the bushes, as they began to think of agreeable and safe ways of accommodating the animals. In fact, their imaginations had run away with them. For the moment they would have to content themselves with a few deer, birds and small mammals; they knew that lions, tigers, giraffes and even gazelles were outside their range. Besides, this was to be a wild-life park – an area of open space where people would be able to roam, 'where the deer and the antelope play'. The larger wilder creatures were the stuff of zoos, and this was not to be a zoo.

But why not? Just as the wild-life park was the next logical step beyond opening the gardens, so keeping a menagerie of caged animals was another natural progression. What was more, there were a number of buildings which were eminently suited to this kind of conversion. There was a two-and-a-half-acre expanse of scrub surrounded by a ten-foot wall – the site of the old mansion house – which had once been a nursery. Now it was a dumping ground and the buildings were derelict. This walled garden would be an ideal zoo site, and it slotted into the total 'visiting area' like the last piece of a jigsaw puzzle. The gardens and the animal paddocks were separated by a half-mile causeway which ran the length of the valley and led into the walled garden; a tour could continue from there past the little church with all its Nelsonalia, and then on along a path past the stables, and through a stone tunnel which led back into the gardens. It was almost as if the fifty-acre site had been designed with this use in mind.

Between them, John, Paddy and the Major were confident that with their combined farming and organizing talents they would be able to administer the venture efficiently, but they did not know much about wild animals. They had never believed in the old principle of cobblers sticking to their lasts, which in view of the number of new skills they had to learn up over the next few weeks was just as well. For the moment at least they needed every bit of help and guidance from the animal experts, and this came from Flamingo Park whence one of the keepers was posted to Cricket as curator. The project was soon embodied in a business contract and Cricket St Thomas Park Ltd was established between the partnership and Associated Pleasure Parks on a fifty-fifty basis. Everybody's place in the venture was clearly delineated. The Major was to manage the wild-life park, under the direction of Flamingo Park, helped by John and Paddy, who would also continue with the farming. The idea had been conceived in June but it was December before much started happening on the estate, although the park was due to open in April.

With the arrival of timber, wire, frames, fences, breeze-blocks and all manner of building materials, began one of the most gruelling periods of hard labour the people on the estate had ever experienced. With them came builders, carpenters, plumbers and painters, but much of the work was done by the regulars on the Cricket payroll, deployed from the fields and milking parlours, who entered into the spirit of the new undertaking with wholehearted enthusiasm. The more they did, the more it seemed still had to be done, and the chances of opening in April became more and more remote. April came, and with it a heat-wave which lasted the next few weeks and in which many a back was tanned by the sun as cages were built, enclosures erected, and the estate was made fit for public consumption. When Paddy installed a notice at the main entrance saying 'Wild Life Park Opening July 1st', the work gained impetus.

It was the walled garden which needed most of the attention. It had to be cleared, levelled off, and replanted, and some of the buildings needed extensive repair. A few outbuildings were converted into cages, and an old greenhouse into an aviary. This area was evidently going to be the focal point of the park, so making it habitable for animals was only half the battle. The other half was making it fit for people. It needed a restaurant, kiosks, swings and slides for children, and above all – the centrepiece of all public playgrounds – loos. These were designed by John. The first loos at Cricket, ironically reincarnated from the ruins of an old potting shed, represent a landmark (one is tempted to say a 'watershed') in John's career in draughtmanship. They were the first he had ever designed and the many which have since come from his drawing board are works of art which he fashions with relish. A queue for the loo, he has learnt, is the symbol of success in the public attraction game. The more loos you have to build, and can keep busy from morning till night, the better business must be.

By the end of May the place was ready to receive the animals. Nobody knew as they put up a fence or built a cage what was going to go inside it. All-purpose compounds were built, which, for all the builders knew, had to take anything from an elephant to a stick-insect. Consequently, when a lorry arrived bearing the first real live animal, all work stopped while the beast was unpacked. A crowd gathered round the lorry and the tension mounted. It fell again abruptly as the creature emerged. It was only a donkey, and not a very good one at that. It stood on the ramp, looked at everybody and started to reverse back into the lorry.

'This is a wild-life park, not a pet shop,' one of the men jeered.

'Knackers' yard up the road,' another instructed the driver.

'Maybe it's a zebra feeling off-colour.'

'I'll soon have his stripes back on,' said the painter.

'It's an ass.'

'Well it takes on to know one.'

The mocking continued as the donkey was led away to its new quarters. The next workbreak was in honour of a consignment of flamingoes. Some of them were standing up in crates, and others had their legs folded in nylon tights – a conventional way of transporting flamingoes, which they did not appear to mind. Once out of the crates and unwound, they stalked down to the lakes stretching their legs like a party of pensioners at a coach-outing comfort stop. The next few arrivals were mostly birds. Among the most impressive of these were two black swans which took to the water like lovers sauntering into the sunset at the end of a film. Lovers they may have been, but not very productive with it – they had never bred. With the deliveries of wild fowl and tropical birds an element of exotic beauty was gradually creeping in, but there was as yet no sign of the 'heavy brigade' – the untamed ferocious creatures which would entitle the place to the name 'WILD-life park'.

Although the park had so few inmates at this early stage the routines of animal care and feeding had to begin in earnest. It was from the outset that the family began to realize that maintaining a routine for the animals would sometimes involve considerable disruption of their own.

From now on it was a frequent occurrence for the phone to ring in the middle of the night.

'Stationmaster here. Your . . . maggots have arrived.' The voice lost a few decibels for the word 'maggots', as if somebody else was in the room he did not want to hear. 'Maggots' is a very difficult word to say in an official voice. In fact, it is not a word you can say with conviction in any tone of voice. It is devoid of poetry, melody and romance, yet maggots are a matter of life and death in a wild-life park. To a bird the phrase 'Grubs-up' is not slang, but a literal statement which contains the promise of survival.

'Ah – the maggots,' John exulted. 'We've been waiting for them.'

The stationmaster now spoke with confidence. It was now confirmed that he had read the smudged label correctly.

'Excuse my asking, sir, but they are marked "Urgent" – what's so urgent about maggots?'

'We're starting a wild-life park.'

There was a moment's silence while the British Rail mind processed the information.

'Starting a bit small, aren't you, sir?'

This was the first of many midnight phone calls from the surrounding stations over the next few days, when various packages marked 'livestock' were dumped on the platform. The arrival of maggots has since become a regular event. During this stocking period animals were arriving thick and fast and one was never quite sure what would be coming when and how. So it was often the stationmaster who had to answer the questions about the packages and crates.

'What's in it?'

'It's alive, sir.'

'A bird?'

'No – it's too big for a bird. It's the size of a dog, and it's furry.'

'What sort of face has it got?'

'I can't see, but a little pointed nose keeps coming out of the air vents.'

'Is it grey?'

'Could be – might be a badger.'

'What sort of noise does it make?'

'Doesn't say much, sir, but it does a lot of scuffling about.'

'Racoon?'

'That's right, sir – says "Raccoon" on the label. That's somewhere in India, isn't it?'

The arrival of a raccoon or any new animal became the high spot of each day, but it always seemed to happen at six in the morning or even earlier. Even so, everybody would turn out to watch, summoned from their beds by the sound of tyres throwing up the gravel, the slamming of doors, the rattle of tailboard chains and cries of 'Where do you want it?' These came from a pair of remarkable Flamingo Park deliverymen, two brothers, who were also a circus act, and, so the rumour had it, had made their name by the one pushing the other in a wheelbarrow on a tight-rope over the Cheddar Gorge.

Everyone would follow the lorry off to the disembarkation point and gather round peering in at crates, like a family clustering round a Christmas tree.

'Wonder what's in this one?'

'Whatever could it be?' assessing the size and shape of the packaging.

'Well, it's not a humming bird,' indicating a six-foot crate.

'Could be a zebra?'

'Too small – more like another donkey.'

'It's a wallaby,' comes a voice with conviction.

A protuding beak or an antler would discredit that diagnosis.

After much heaving, hammering and crowbarring, the crates would be sufficiently demolished to allow for the emergence of the whole animal. Everybody would stand back oo-ing and ah-ing in wonder like spectators at a fire-work display, always expecting more to happen than actually did. This was always a traumatic moment. For the spectators it was in most cases their first view of a wallaby, or an eland or wapiti at close quarters. For the animals it was

39

their first view of their new home. Some were over-cautious and had to be coaxed out of the crates. The deer would delight in their new freedom and skip about, happy to see their companions again. They could not believe that the whole of their enclosure was all for them, and congregated in a huddle in one corner until everybody had gone away.

No such inhibitions restrained the new emu, which strode out haughtily, turned, and bowed, and then started off on a lap of honour in its enclosure. Another superior creature was one of the llamas, which arrived loose in a cattle truck. When the ramp was let down, it drew itself up to its full height, and stood there like a knight about to cross his castle drawbridge on the way to the Crusades. He then stepped down into his pasture with immense dignity and never looked round. Its mate ruined that majestic effect, stumbling out backwards. The three dingoes – which look much like ordinary mongrel dogs – got much the same reception as the donkey.

The release of the wild fowl, cranes, peacocks and aviary birds was uneventful. They waddled, stalked or fluttered off giving no appearance of being either impressed or distressed. The monkeys took to their cages like children to an adventure playground and were far too busy swinging from branch to bar and back to branch by way of suspended rubber tyres, to notice for the moment that their new playing area had impenetrable boundaries.

A number of wallabies arrived before their enclosure was quite ready, and had to be housed temporarily in a smaller pen, while the final touches were made. The way to transport a wallaby over a short distance is not to let it leap along under its own steam but to hold its tail and steer it in the right direction. For the 'driver' the sensation is like trying to steer a powered barrow with a square wheel, and the sight of six of the staff bounding across the lawn, each attached to a wallaby, looked like an event from 'It's a Knockout'.

The most enthusiastic arrival was that of the zebra. He could not wait to get out of the crate and into his enclosure, and once the slide was up he shot straight out, cantered across the paddock and jumped into the lake. This was one of the most valuable animals in the collection so far, and, seeing his life endangered, the attendant staff wasted no time in wading waist deep into the water after it. The zebra waited until as many people as possible were as wet as possible and then trotted out again with an impish expression on his face. He thus became one of the few park animals which has even assisted in its own salvaging manoeuvres. They normally panic and struggle, thereby making any operation, be it transportation or medical treatment, far more difficult.

The zebra was thereafter regarded as a doubtful character, but redeemed himself in the following months, something which could not be said for the bison. His arrival at the park was probably one of the least alarming moments of his whole life at Cricket. His first appearance was attended by the customary formalities and entourage, and by more than usual excitement, since a bison was a rarity, and had that element of wildness which the other animals lacked. But when he eventually emerged every palpitating heart missed a beat. Out came the shabbiest, ugliest and most repellent brute creation could ever have devised. One got the feeling that he had been kept alive up to this point in the hope that some wild-life park would open where he could be off-loaded. Cricket had obliged. He was almost certainly a runt animal with enough poundage and all the obligatory appurtenances to qualify him as a bison, yet so threadbare and out of condition that he could only just have passed. He coughed wheezily, lumbered slowly down the ramp and took up a position a few yards away from his nauseated welcoming committee. Then, turning round and giving the group quite the dirtiest look imaginable, he bellowed a warning, like a sergeant-major striking the fear of God into a platoon of raw recruits:

'You 'orrible lot – you 'aven't 'eard the end of me. I'm goin' to make men out of you so let's get that clear from the start you 'ideous shower. What are you . . . ?'

Sergeant-majors usually temper their initial unpleasantness as time goes on and you can accuse them of being two-faced. To the bison's credit, he would be innocent of that charge. He was one-faced – and this was it. The group dispersed uncertainly with their legs quivering, leaving the evil-tempered beast to its own devices.

Now the place could really qualify as a 'wild'-life park, a classification it was already entitled to if by 'wild', 'free-roaming' was meant. But what would the public expect of a wild-life park? Lions? Tigers? Giraffes? Gorillas? People would be familiar with zoos, and they might have been to Longleat, which had only recently opened with its famous lions, but with wild-life parks being a new feature of the British landscape, there was nothing else from which they could form any preconceptions. Yet some might come with an exaggerated notion of what a wild-life park should be, and might find themselves disappointed by this modest collection of relatively harmless creatures.

The Major had been meticulous about creating the right impression, anxious not to inflate public expectations in the publicity which was now going out all over the West Country. The office had produced a glossy brochure, in which all the animals and birds were well illustrated and documented, and which made no claims which could not be substantiated. Most brochures for zoos and parks have a picture of their star exhibit on the cover, and a magnificent picture of Cricket's impressive wapiti – its antlered head borne proudly aloft surveying the park from a woodland ridge – seemed to set the right tone.

Yet, for some reason, the brochure did not give quite the right picture. The fault lay not with the brochure but with the place itself. Over the last few weeks creatures of one sort or another had been arriving in their hundreds, and everybody felt that they must have the place well and truly stocked by now. But they had been dispersed over such a vast area that one could look down the valley and hardly see any signs of the animals which had been released into it. For a start, most of the deer had taken to the woods and were not to be seen again for twelve months. The wallabies, which had looked conspicuous enough when they arrived, now looked tiny, and tended to congregate in a far corner of their enclosure out of sight. The flamingoes, crested cranes, storks, pelicans, swans and wild fowl had settled for detached accommodation, and, spread over such a wide lakeside area, they failed to create the intended colourful impact of a cosmopolitan colony. Between the aviaries and the cages in the walled garden at one end of the valley, and the bison and zebra at the other, there was a half-mile walk of what appeared to be uninhabited virgin territory. Certainly it was beautiful in itself, but a visitor does not appreciate flora if he is out looking for fauna.

Even the walled garden itself looked sparsely populated; the aviaries were well stocked, but otherwise there were only a couple of rhesus monkeys, a pair of spot-nose monkeys ,the dingoes, the raccoons and the odd peacock. Even with the new restaurant, a shop and a children's playground, that two and a half acres looked pretty desolate. With only a week to go before opening, there was not much one could do about this situation short of buying and enclosing or caging many more animals. A few gestures were made by way of 'filling up' with a few farm animals. A number of indignant calves, pigs, and lambs and a rabbit or two found themselves reassigned to deputize for wilder creatures in the hope that they might snarl a bit and pass themselves off as something more interesting. Even when they threw up a scaffolding frame on the lawn outside the restaurant and flung a strawberry net over it, to impound a few cranes and sacred ibises, the walled garden still looked empty. One corner particularly cried out for some kind of embellishment, and it was Paddy, who was staring at that bare expanse of wall with what must have been X-ray eyes, who hit on an inspired idea. The other side of it was the home farm milking parlour; it had had a ready-made attraction behind it all the time. If the wall was knocked down and a glass panel substituted, people would be able to look straight down into the central pit between the two lines of cows' udders and watch the milking.

It was a master stroke and the job was done within the day. Soon there was not only a glass panel, but also a covered viewing gallery with a sloping floor so that people of all heights could stand four deep and see the milking. It was John's younger brother, Stephen, who was that day deputizing for the regular herdsman, who gave the first public milking display and put on his cleanest overalls for the pilot performance. John, Paddy and a few others were standing in the viewing gallery at the matinée milking time. Through the glass they saw Stephen stride into the pit like a circus ringmaster walk down towards the viewers and bow. He then mouthed an announcement which they could not hear, but lip-read as something like 'And now, ladies and gentlemen . . .' If any sound had penetrated the panel they were now laughing too much to hear it. With that Stephen turned and skipped up to the other end of the parlour in time to some non-existent music, and threw open the door to bring on his guest artistes. It was 'Stephen and his Liberty Cows'. The cattle filed in lethargically, eyeing Stephen suspiciously as they took their positions in the stalls, where they turned and stared horrified at the faces peering at them through the glass. Stephen was now back in the pit and the act took off on another track. Taking a pair of rubber gloves off the rail, he came up to the glass and held them out for the audience's inspection, showing both sides, turning them inside-out and blowing into them. He then blew one of them up, and with expansive gestures compared his fingered balloon with the udder and teats of the first cow. But she did not like the look of this departure from the normal routine and recoiled as Stephen approached. It was time to get on with the job, and Stephen bowed to the audience and, with a twisting wrist gesture, indicated that the spectators should switch off or change channel. The gallery was ahoot with laughter and wild with applause.

Had anyone had time to sit back and survey the fruits of

their labours of the last few weeks they would have been well pleased. It was not that the place yet looked like the idyllic park it was to become, but it was considerably more presentable than it had been before. Where it had once been dishevelled and unkempt it was now 'hevelled' and 'kempt', but that was about as far as it went. The estate had not yet attained the status of a public exhibition, but it would be no good saying to a disgruntled customer 'Ah – but you should have seen what it was like before'. But there was no reason why paying visitors should be dissatisfied. The publicity had stated simply that this was a wild-life park in which lived deer, bison, zebra, dingo, emu, rhea, monkey, raccoon, flamingo, stork, crane, peacock and twelve varieties of wild duck. This was all perfectly true, so what more would anybody be wanting? They would have to wait and see.

Placing all the animals was an operation which had called for skill and judgement. It was obvious which animals were destined for cages, and which birds for the aviaries, but it was not so clear which creatures could be safely let loose together in the parklands. Ideally the aim would be to have all the animals and water birds living together in harmony in the one enclosure, but this was plainly wishful thinking. Could be the bison be persuaded to be civil to a flamingo? Would a zebra and a rhea find that they had much in common? What would a llama make of a wallaby as a room-mate? Initially it was not worth the risk of finding out, so a certain amount of segregation was imperative.

The vexed question of getting the 'lion to lie down with the lamb' reminded Paddy of another page in a children's puzzle book – the brain-teaser about the fox, the chicken and the bag of corn. 'There was once a farmer who lived by a river, and had to ferry across a fox, a chicken and a bag of corn but there was only room for one passenger in the boat at a time. He made three crossings. How did he manage it without leaving the fox on either bank to eat the chicken, or the chicken alone to eat the bag of corn?' The Cricket quandary was from now on to be an enlarged and far more convoluted version of this riddle – how to get so many different creatures with their various life-styles, territorial requirements, diets, affinities and hostilities to co-exist peaceably without infringing each other's natural rights and freedoms. But now the Cricket estate had to brace itself to admit another element into the riddle which the farmer with his fox, chicken and bag of corn did not have to contend with. It was a common species, and at this moment the only conspicuous absentee – *Homo sapiens*.

Cricket St Thomas Wild Life Park now opened its gates to the public.

3

The Secret Valley Unveiled

One brush-stroke of emulsion converted the notice 'Wild Life Park Opening July 1st' to 'Wild Life Park Open'. A promise was a promise, and it was 1 July. One way or another it was going to be a telling day and the weather augured well for it. Arthur Lewis – a retired florist who was one of the many locals who rallied to the cry for help – was stationed with rolls of cloakroom tickets and a till in a little hut which went by the name of 'Pay Here'. By ten o'clock Paddy, John and the Major were hovering about looking anxious. The womenfolk were in the restaurant brewing coffee and buttering bread. A few volunteers had donned white coats and stood beyond the paybox ready to marshal cars into the parking area. Cars? They waited in apprehensive silence for fifteen minutes, staring hopefully up the valley to the top of the drive. Twenty minutes. At last a little estate car appeared at the end of the tunnel of trees. It disappeared in a dip in the road where there was a fork leading to the western exit and was never seen again.

'Blast.'

'Got to do something about those short-cut merchants. That bit's private.'

Another half hour passed. Paddy had worn down a patch of grass with his pacing up and down, and was just starting on another patch. Then another vehicle appeared at the top of the drive, emerged from the tunnel, disappeared into the dip and re-appeared. It rattled up the road towards them and ground to a halt. It was an old van full of children.

'How much is it?' asked a harrassed-looking father in a tartan cap.

'Ten shillings,' said Arthur. 'You've got a bargain with that lot.'

'Anything off for commercial vehicles?'

The reception committee laughed. It was their first taste of public parsimony. They were to learn soon enough that the old tradition of barter was not dead yet.

'What do we do – drive through and keep the windows shut?' enquired the wife from the other side of the cab.

'Park over there and walk – you won't get eaten.'

They seemed unconvinced but drove on.

Another car had drawn up, followed by a motor bike.

'Look – a queue,' said Paddy enthusiastically.

As Arthur took the money, several more cars were beginning to appear. Confident that they were now in business, the management withdrew to get on with their own things. Paddy got into the Land-Rover and made off up the drive against the line of traffic, peering down at the occupants of the cars as he passed.

'People seem to have vast families these days,' he mused, noting that every car was bursting with people. Arriving at the top of the drive, he looked at his notice with satisfaction.

Cricket St Thomas Wild Life Park
Entrance 10/- per car

Then he noticed the verges were crammed with parked cars. It was a moment or two before he figured out what was going on. People were parking their cars, getting into somebody else's, making a deal and all getting in for ten shillings. The park had only been open an hour and already it was losing a fortune. He leapt out of the Land-Rover, covered up the offending '10/- per car' with an old fertilizer bag, and swung round the Land-Rover back down the drive, but only to get caught in the queue. At the first gate he turned off into a field and drove furiously cross-country making a bee-line for the pay-box. Somewhere in that queue were some gatecrashers who had to be intercepted.

Nobody admitted to this illegal entry and Paddy's case was very difficult to prove, but an impromptu board meeting approved the substitution of a charge per head for a charge per car. It was a day or two before the revised toll could be introduced, and meanwhile one of the white coats was deployed to the top of the drive to ensure that all cars which entered the main gate got as far as the pay-box.

By midday the cars were coming in a steady stream. The Major viewed them with satisfaction from the lawn in front of his house adjoining the approach road. He conceded that the gratifying numbers might be due to a combination of initial curiosity and 'beginner's luck', but harboured an earnest hope that he was wrong, and that such interest could be sustained as time went on. Some of it, he averred, might be nothing to do with the wild-life park. Hitherto, Cricket St Thomas had been a secret valley. For most local people it was a blind-spot in their knowledge of the neighbourhood. Everybody knew that 'down there' was a beautiful valley, a historic mansion, and unspoilt piece of old England, but few people had been allowed past its lodges. It was impenetrably private. Suddenly all was being revealed.

The car park was now full and vehicles were spilling over on to grassland, chrome and glass gleaming in the sun. A peacock had joined a family picnic. The gardens and paddock thoroughfares were dotted with small groups of ambling visitors, stopping, pointing, taking photographs and being tugged onwards by little children.

'Goodbye,' said a mynah bird in its aviary just inside the entrance to the walled garden to a family which had just arrived. 'Hello,' it said to a party which was just leaving.

'Round here, you don't know if you're coming or going,' said a humorist, a joke which was to be heard so often outside that aviary that the mynah birds might one day be able to crack it for themselves.

The animals themselves were intrigued by this unaccountable influx of bipeds. Boldest among them was the emu which came right up to its barrier and craned its neck over the bar to investigate people's coat buttons. The monkeys showed off most of their tricks, and the zebra was interested enough to approach the perimeters of the enclosure, though it kept its distance. The raccoons paced around anxiously but the wallabies were not taking much notice and congregated in a group in the middle of their paddock. The bison couldn't care less.

The squeals of delight from the children on the swings, the tings from the till in the shop and the flushing of cisterns in the lavatories denoted that everything was in working order and functioning properly. At lunchtime the restaurant had filled up and was doing good trade, mostly in coffees and soft drinks for people who had brought their own lunches, not wanting to risk the hazards of an untried catering establishment. In one corner a waitress was attending to an irate customer complaining about the nutritional value of a sausage roll.

'I opened it up and look,' he thundered, pointing at two pitiful knobs of meat at either end of the roll. 'It's hollow.'

'I'll get you another,' said the waitress cordially.

'Who's the boss round here? Who lives in the castle?'

'Some people called Taylor,' replied the waitress.

'Well, that's who I'm going to complain to.'

'I'll get the manageress.'

That 'waitress' was Doreen. All meals served, she repaired back to the 'castle' for her own lunch and an hour or two off-duty. Rosemary had laid the lunch table out on the terrace, where they could look out on the gardens and see the visitors roaming about.

As they ate their way through a chicken salad they became aware of an unanticipated presence. The sound of trodden gravel attracted their attent on to the approach of uninvited guests.

The public 'trail' had taken the visitors along a lower path away from the house, but ever since they had been having lunch visitors had been taking a detour up on to the top path which took them past the terrace where they were stopping to 'rubberneck' at the lunch party. The family was itself an exhibit. It was a horrifying thought that the house and its occupants were regarded as a zoo annexe, but an understandable misconception. The brochure had given the visitors to understand that the house was on show, and there were certainly no notices to the contrary, and no barriers to indicate where the public sector ended and the private sector began.

'We'll have to put up a sign about this,' whispered Rosemary out of the corner of her mouth, then smiling weakly and nodding at the riveted spectators.

John made a note of it in his pad. 'What shall we say?'

'Proprietor Ferocious – This Animal is Dangerous. Do Not Stare,' he suggested.

'Well, two can play at this game,' said Rosemary, getting up from the table. 'Let's go and look at them.'

It was as well they did, because as they strode through the park incognito, finding the visitors much more interesting than the animals themselves, John suddenly noticed an absentee.

'Where in heaven's name is that bison?' he gasped.

The bison pen was empty.

'Oh no,' he blurted out, thinking that if there was one animal he never wanted loose, particularly on the first day, it was that evil-tempered bison.

'What's that down there?' Rosemary was pointing into the lake at the bottom of the paddock. A pair of horns were bobbing Excalibur-like on the surface of the water in the middle of the lake.

'He's just having a swim.'

They stood staring at the horns for what seemed a very long time.

'Do you think he ought to be having a swim?'

'Perhaps he's a water buffalo.'

'They didn't tell us he was. Even so, he should have surfaced by now.'

'Water buffalo can't breathe underwater, can they?'

John referred mentally to all his reading up on animals.

'I don't think so.'

It took some moments for it to sink in that they were confronted with their first animal emergency. John leapt over the fence and ran down to the lake. The animal still showed no inclination to surface, but the horns began to lurch about, which John took to be a signal that down below a ton of brawn might perhaps be struggling for survival.

'Get Henry with the tractor and the winch,' he yelled to Rosemary.

Tearing a branch from a tree, he stepped into the shallows of the lake and prodded the bison with it. Then, calculating where the animal's chin might be, he made what he thought would be an ineffectual attempt to heave its head up. Surprisingly it worked and a snout appeared out of the water, gasping. There he held it until the bison was breathing again regularly and gratefully. Realizing that the beast was undoubtedly stuck, John ventured right up to it, and held its head. Soon the tractor was chugging into the paddock, and the winch cable was secured to the bison's horns. The tractor revved up and edged away up the slope and the bison was slowly but surely dragged ashore. As he was detaching the cable from the horns, John lost his usual fear of the animal, feeling that this daring and selfless rescue entitled him to a measure of respect and gratitude from the bison. But not a bit of it; as soon as he was freed he took a few paces backwards, bellowed, put his head down and went into a full-blooded charge. John just managed to skip out of the way, and while the bison turned for another assault he was able to slip behind the tractor, which provided enough cover as it retreated towards the gate.

'I'll leave you in there next time,' roared John from the safety of the other side of the barrier. He meant it, too.

The rest of the family had rushed down to the lake and had caught the tail-end of the incident.

'That bison doesn't know what's good for it,' John complained. 'It's determined to be difficult.'

'Of course – he's a Taurean,' said Doreen, a great believer in astrology.

A crowd of visitors had gathered – for them this was the high spot of the day. Realizing that they were in the presence of the management, they wasted no time in giving their opinions of the park.

'Nice place you've got here,' said an appreciative lady.

'Got any camels, mister?' blurted out a small boy.

'Not at the moment.'

'When will they be here?'

'Maybe soon. Have you seen the monkeys?' said John treading on safer ground.

'Saw one. It didn't do anything funny.'

People were looking at John as he walked back up the bank. He felt he had to say something; after all, they were his guests.

'Have you seen everything?' he asked a man in a tartan cap. It was the first visitor of the morning.

'Everything? Haven't seen anything yet. I thought you might at least have an elephant.'

'Camels and elephants,' John noted – his first bit of market research. And perhaps they should lay on a bison rescue every day as a main attraction.

Paddy went back to the restaurant where the kitchen was full of about twenty women drinking cups of tea surrounded by piles of gleaming plates, cups and cutlery. The washing up was a good job done, but did it need that many people? He started to do some rough calculations in his head. Multiplying the going rate for washing up by twenty, he went out into the car park to count the vehicles. Thirty-two. Twenty had left, which meant a total of fifty-two at ten shillings apiece, plus profits on meals and ice-creams, but less animal food bills, staff wages . . . Figures filled his head for the rest of the day.

'We're in business.' It was the Major who announced it, getting up from the floor of the park office in his house, where he had spent the early evening kneeling surrounded by cash-boxes, piles of notes and loose change and pages of sums. That night the proprietors drank a toast to their fifty-two car loads.

The heatwave was still holding out the following day, as everybody took up their stations to receive another invasion of visitors. Paddy, who was rehinging a gate halfway up the drive, started to count the cars as they came in, but soon gave up. They were coming in an unrelenting torrent. It seemed incredible.

'How many, Arthur?' he shouted from the Land-Rover as he passed the pay-box at lunchtime.

'A hundred and sixteen.'

'Get away.'

'It's true – look,' Arthur replied, holding up a wad of pound notes. 'Where are you off to?'

'I'm going to the house for lunch.'

'There won't be any lunch there. Every woman in the place is up at the restaurant. They can't keep up with it.'

Paddy swung the Land-Rover round and drove back to the the walled garden. Within minutes he had a soggy tea-towel in his hand and had probably dried up the same plate four times – after four different meals had been eaten off it – before he got any lunch himself. At the end of the day the family had to retrieve all their own plates and cutlery which had been commandeered by the restaurant. They had underestimated the number of visitors they could expect. Being farmers and used to a seven-day working week, they were not acquainted with the ways of 'the world and his wife'. They did not know that the traditional family outing was a Sabbath activity, and that they should have expected far more visitors on the Sunday than the Saturday. It came as a shock. The streams of cars did not abate, and by the end of the weekend 1,250 people had been round the park.

Nobody could believe it. That evening the family sat on the terrace in stunned silence, smiling to themselves with satisfaction. As the sun went down John and Rosemary walked down the sloping lawn to the Magnolia Walk where they could look over the whole valley.

'Well done, animals,' said John.

A lone quack acknowledged the compliment.

'You know those black swans,' said Rosemary.

'Yes.'

'Didn't you say they'd never bred before?'

'That's right.'

'Well, look,' Rosemary pointed to a clump of reeds in the shallows of the lake. The female swan was putting out from the bank – followed by three cygnets.

4

Teething Troubles

Those black swans continued to multiply – and in more senses than one. Their breeding was taken as a good omen, and thereafter a black swan became the emblem of the park – its silhouette appearing on the notepaper, the vehicles, the car stickers, and once in later years on a raft entered by the park for a charity raft regatta. A sudden preoccupation with the emblem was the first indication that there was now time to consider the finer points of running a wild-life park. Until now every unit of manpower, money, time and energy had gone into providing the essentials – animals, loos and refreshments.

There was no knowing that the initial flood of visitors of the first weekend was not a freak wave. Time would tell, but the question could not be left to time alone. If the first flush of popularity and interest was to flourish it would be by the efforts of the park, coupled with word-of-mouth reports from those first 1,250 visitors starting a snowball of recommendation. Judging from some of their comments so far this could not be guaranteed, and there was still much to do to ensure that the next inflow would be more satisfied, so that subsequent visitors would be positively impressed. Visitors continued to come in midweek trickles, followed by weekend torrents. What grumblings there were concerned the choice of animals. No amount of explanation could convince everybody that lions, tigers, elephants, giraffes, camels and rhinoceroses were not the mainstays of a wild-life park. For some, the handsome array of birds and the deer, and the odd monkey and racoon were only a poor substitute for the 'Big League'. It all seemed a bit tame. But the park was now in business, and, realizing that it would have to make concessions to public opinion, the Major started negotiations to acquire an elephant.

Collecting animals is not unlike collecting stamps. At the outset you have to make do with other people's 'swaps'. Cricket, in its early stages, was having to make do with the surplus stock from other zoos and parks and certainly the bison had that 'perforated' look about it. It was an odd selection of animals. The park was well endowed with birds and deer, but the rarer animals were indeed in short supply. The monkeys, raccoons, coatimundis, porcupines, zebra and bison were fine attractions in themselves, but the odd mixture gave the impression that the collection was far from complete. Furthermore, the deer in the parkland had not yet recovered from their initial shyness and were still in hiding. The 'wild' area looked sparsely inhabited. But most people were prepared to accept the park for what it was, enjoying the gardens, the birds, the church and the walk as much as anything.

One astonishing success was the popularity of the milking parlour. At four o'clock the viewing gallery in the corner of the walled garden would be packed with people who stared transfixed as the herdsman went through his milking routine – by now a more subdued version. The realization that even in this rural area there were many adults who had never seen cows being milked, and even thought that milk grew in bottles, came as a surprise. But the looks of amazement on some of the faces indicated that some visitors were city dwellers – coming from distant towns looking in on their West-Country tours. Word was getting about. Even the little cluster of pens containing the 'fillers' – the sheep, lambs, pigs and calves – were getting an unexpected share of attention.

'What's that funny black-and-white thing?' said one man, staring into a pen which the management had thought they could reasonably leave unlabelled.

'I'm not sure, but I think it's a baby cow,' ventured his

wife. Nobody could be sure what these domestic animals thought they were masquerading as, but they were certainly entering into the spirit of the thing.

'I think we must drink calves' milk at school,' a little girl deduced, coming out of the milking bay and staring into the pen containing a charolais calf.

'What do you mean – calves' milk?'

'Well, at school we have it in the little bottles.'

Once Cricket was established as a wild-life park, animals started arriving from strange quarters, heralded by the short, timid 'ding' of the office doorbell. A small boy would arrive on the doorstep with a python coiled round him, asking for a home for it. Up to this point he had kept it in the bath in his home in a Bristol suburb. A couple of Malabar squirrels came from a retired army colonel who had brought them back from India as retirement mascots, but could not look after them. A small monkey was brought in 'on probation' by an old lady, under pressure from neighbours whose thatched roof the monkey had been systematically shredding. One man even brought a stuffed and mounted moose's head, which was not something which could be put in an enclosure with tact. Contributions to the collection were always welcomed, although there was one exception. That donation was Pimple – a red deer – which had been hand-reared by a woman who was moving house. There would be no room for Pimple in her new home. As it turned out there was ultimately no room for Pimple at Cricket either; he was the most vicious and contemptible creature the park had ever had to contend with.

Yet at this stage – several months into the first season – every little bit helped. One was particularly grateful to any of the animals which made themselves conspicuous and sociable to the visitors. Among the most gregarious of them was the eland. Although he was old and had the tatty look of a swap about him, he could be relied upon to run about and turn up where visitors happened to be, thereby giving the impression of a herd. He was the star turn and knew it. In the first couple of months he had been perfectly willing to make himself amenable to a certain number of visitors, but he had never had to cope with a British bank holiday. As activity all around him reached fever pitch to prepare for what could be an unprecedented number of people, he must have sensed that he was going to have to be more sociable than usual. He began to get nervous, like an actor on the eve of a well-tried touring production's opening in the West End. His stage fright was more than flesh and blood could stand, and the following morning he had a heart attack and died. It was Cricket's first taste of tragedy. His timing was singularly inconvenient, but the show had to go on. By the time John and Paddy found him it was too late to find an understudy, so they picked up the corpse and dragged it to a far corner of an enclosure where, propped up against a tree, the moribund eland was on display as usual. As in life, so in death.

'It is as he would have wished it,' said Paddy unconvinced.

The eland's herd impressions were much missed, and it was several weeks before he had a replacement which was the genuine article. The later mid-season arrivals included a whole herd of highland cattle. They were attractive beasts, solidly built with shaggy coats of reddish brown, and huge handlebar horns with a span of about five feet on the largest of them. There were fifteen of them in all, including several calves, and they looked sufficiently fierce to give the valley a look of the wild. At last the place was looking fuller. The cattle created this impression of fullness by continually trotting about their enclosure. Some would follow the visitors as they walked along the other side of the fence as a distraction, while others would sweep round to meet them at the other end of the paddock, and no one would know that they were in fact the same ones. Despite their fierce appearance, they were ordinary cattle, and did not warrant the strictest security, with the result that they were continually getting out. Recapturing the odd steer became part of the normal routine, but after a time they became too adventurous and were continually having to be rounded up several miles away. One weekend the whole herd got out, and were rampaging all over the estate, and being unduly uncooperative with one of the keepers, who spent a whole morning trying to get them together. His ultimate success presented a nasty moment for Arthur Lewis, who was stationed in the pay-box, peaceably counting the takings. Hearing a shout of 'Arthur!', he looked out to see the entire herd bearing down on him in a full-blooded stampede. The pay-box was only a flimsy wooden structure and no bastion against an onslaught of such tonnage; all Arthur could do was to crouch down on the floor and prepare himself for an abrupt demise. But the charge left the little shack intact, and both Arthur and the pay-box lived to see another day.

To all appearances the infant park seemed to be thriving, but it was constantly suffering setbacks which were jeopardizing its survival. Its birth had been to some extent premature. Its nine-month gestation period had not produced a fully formed embryo, and there was still much to do which should have been done before it opened. One of these was to win official recognition for its existence, and getting planning permission was one of its most irritating teething troubles. The sudden emergence of a wild-life park in the neighbourhood was not a routine matter for the local authority, and nobody was quite sure how to deal with it. Applying for planning permission was an afterthought, the fact that it was already in operation adding to the confusion of already confounded officials. It was as well the family had found out that a water authority plan to flood the whole valley for a reservoir had been abandoned. The application had to be treated as a special case, and the ensuing negotiations and inspections seemed to be delaying a decision indefinitely. Fears that the neighbourhood would be terrorized by the rampages of escaped lions or gorillas wrinkled a brow or two among the local worthies who had to be reassured. Sub-committees concerned about road hazards and congestion by queueing traffic on the A30 had to be placated; rating authorities which might see the park as a good source of revenue had to be softened. Arguments for and against echoed through the council chambers, while the park waited on tenterhooks for a decision.

In the end the main point at issue was the 'Cricket St Thomas Wild Life Park' sign at the end of the drive. As far as the council was concerned, it was too big and conspicuous and it would cause a distraction to passing motorists. If they allowed it to stay, then they would have to permit every bed-and-breakfast establishment to flaunt notices five foot square, which would be an obstacle to passing lorries. Wild-life parks were a new feature of the British landscape, and the law had not caught up. For the moment, in the eyes of the law, they were subject to the same regulations as guest houses, a classification which did not, in practice, make sense. Nor, incidentally, did other legislation which worked in the park's favour. One has to have a licence to be born, to marry, to keep a dog, to own a gun, to drive a car, to run a restaurant, to sell ice-cream, to purvey cigarettes and liquor – all designed to keep personal and public life tidy and to protect the public from abuses and dangers. One activity for which one does not have to have a licence is keeping a collection of wild animals and allowing people to mingle with them. After months of deliberation the park was officially sanctioned – but only for five years. After that, said the authorities, the land would have to revert to its former state. As this would mean planting weeds and reconstructing derelict buildings, it was not a stricture which could be taken too seriously. The management pressed on as if Cricket Wild Life Park was for ever. Its operation was becoming a matter of routine but there was no let up in the pace of activity. The old tradition for self-sufficiency on the estate was again coming into its own. There was a job for every man, woman and child on the estate, particularly when harvest-time, which usually syphons off every bit of casual labour, coincided with the peak visiting periods in the park. Sunny days were a godsend to both. While the menfolk were in the fields, in the workshops or in the milking parlours, the womenfolk were selling ice-cream and souvenirs, cooking and washing up in the restaurant, and the older children were supervising the car parking. There were seventy people on the pay-roll, and thirty families depended on the farms and park for their livelihood. Rosemary was by this time several months into her second pregnancy and spent most of the summer in an activity unsuited to her condition, bending down to delve into the bowels of the deep freeze – one of the primary working positions of ice-cream selling.

For Paddy that first summer was a chapter of accidents. On a routine inspection of the parkland he drove a Mini to the bottom of one of the paddocks by the lake, and got out to give a llama a check-up. As he walked along the bank he heard an ominous splash behind him and looked round to see the Mini rolling into the lake until the water was all but over the roof. Henry, the denizen of the winch, rose to this occasion as gallantly as he had rescued the bison, but not before Paddy had waded in to take the Mini handbrake off. His next disaster was to turn a combine-harvester over, but the casualty of this episode was John, who was nowhere near it at the time. Driving towards the house, John saw the combine on the distant slopes and noticed that its red stripe, which normally ran horizontally round the machine, was now vertical. After checking his impression with binoculars, he rushed to the scene, to find the upturned harvester embedded in the hillside, the driver's seat inextricably buried; but there was no sign of a driver, no trail left by a broken body dragging itself through the straw, no sound of agonized whimpers from any nearby thicket. Ashenfaced, he returned dolefully to the house to find Paddy happily knocking back a glass of brandy, a tipple which John was happy to share. It was Henry with his ubiquitous winch who, by righting the capsized harvester, closed another fateful episode.

These little sideshows were not part of the public entertainment – they were events from which the people of the estate derive a certain amount of amusement in hindsight. They contribute to the Cricket folklore, and to the store of adventures which make life on the estate constantly lively and exciting. In such a whirlpool of diverse activity it was already becoming clear that nothing was so predictable as the unpredictable. Whatever happened to shatter the day-to-day routines, it all had to be taken as part of the day's work. They had to be ready for anything. Arthur Lewis, for one, had his share of excitement. He had already visualized himself being trampled into oblivion by the stampeding highland cattle, and his sense of security in his little pay-box was about to take another jolt. It was the end of the season, by which time he had admitted 18 000 cars and coaches, and some 60 000 people. The omen of the black swans had proved true. As the last cars were filtering away, Arthur 'locked up', slinging a rope across the drive between a mounting on the pay-box and the fence on the other side of the road. The Major then drove up in his car to enquire about the day's takings, parking it abreast of the rope which hung limply across the front bumper. By the time Arthur had waylaid him with his ever-colourful descriptions of the day's visitors, the Major had forgotten the rope was there. Nor could he see it when he got back into the car. As Arthur watched the car drive off, he was not a little startled to find that both he and the pay-box were also on the move. He suddenly found himself hurtling through a ninety-degree arc and sprawling in a cascade of loose change as the pay-box broke loose from its moorings and landed at the horizontal. Old soldier that he was, Arthur had been trained in the correct procedure for such situations. He lay to attention and saluted.

If the birth of the young black swans at the beginning of the season had been taken as a good omen for the fortunes of the park, what would the augurers make of the cataclysmic demolition of the pay-box at the end?

5

Sealions in the Fountain

In a wild-life park time itself is on the loose. It does not pass by as an unwavering sequence of days, weeks, months and years, conveniently punctuated by weekends, holidays and festivals. The opening and closing of the 'season' are about the only events which are governed by the calendar, and only the visitors and the shop and office staffs abide by that. The timetable of the keepers is prescribed by the feeding and breeding patterns of the animals – each to its own chronology, and none switching off at the end of the season. A walk across the park would take one through several time zones. Animals are no respecters of routines, schedules and programmes except when it suits them. The people on the estate have to fall in with their several requirements. For instance, John's life is plotted not by seasons, dates and time of day, but by events, which he dates by the arrival and departure of animals, the construction of a new building or the demolition of an old. Paddy's activities are ruled by the demands of the farms – by the life-cycles of herds and crops and fluctuations of the market. Doreen's unit for the measurement of time is the family, a gauge on which births, marriages, deaths, anniversaries and dental appointments are the gradations. For the children, life is fragmented by terms, holidays and mealtimes.

One spring morning Paddy burst into the kitchen during breakfast.

'Come quickly, the elephant is lose in the garage.'

Everybody leapt up and rushed outside.

'It's breaking up all the cars.'

Throwing open the garage door, the family found no sign of a rampaging elephant and no damage to any cars.

'April Fool!' chortled Paddy behind them.

It was a mean trick to play, exploiting two soft spots in the wild-life-park mentality. First, in the timeless ferment of events, the fact that it was 1 April was almost certain to have escaped everybody else's attention. Secondly, no matter how outrageous the emergency he had concocted, it would be believable and his dupes would be duty-bound to take it seriously and respond. As there were many times when they were suddenly alerted in this way, this false alarm was not particularly appreciated. They had to seize periods of relaxation where they could, and there was always a fair chance that these would be short-lived. Doreen had a home-spun saying, 'All work and no play, makes Jack a dull boy', which she would reel out whenever anyone showed signs of wilting under the pressure. Everybody had to take relaxing seriously. Her own way of switching off was writing and illustrating children's stories. One of these was about a squirrel and a rabbit visiting a wild-life park. One evening she was reading a few verses of it to the family circle.

'The notice said "Wild Life Park – open today. Rabbits and squirrels do not have to pay".'

'They would if I was on the gate,' Paddy interjected.

'Oh, surely not,' Doreen protested, quite believing that the situation might arise.

'We get enough gate-crashers as it is. What about all those ton-up lads who slipped in the back way last year?'

'It wasn't last year,' Rosemary corrected. 'It was about the same time the camel broke its leg, and that was more than a year ago.'

'It was just after Grandma died,' Doreen averted.

John had other ideas.

'No, it wasn't. I remember taking one of those motor bikes and hiding it in the stables – so it must have been before the elephant was there. That's at least three years ago. By the way, we're getting the other elephant next week.'

'What are we paying for it?' asked Paddy anxiously.

'Fourteen hundred.'

'Good Lord. And here's Mother wanting to let rabbits and squirrels in free.'

Doreen reappraised her manuscript.

'I can't say rabbits and squirrels get in reduced, it doesn't rhyme.'

'Put "DO have to pay" – that rhymes.'

By 1972, John was in command of the wild-life park operation, and when the Flamingo Park overlords withdrew from the partnership Cricket was on its own. Not only had the park bought up its existing stock, but it was now continually adding to the collection. The 'family' had grown with the addition of Twiggy, the elephant, a young camel called Fariq, some pumas, leopards, lynx, peccaries and civet cats, and an assortment of monkeys – Japanese, Diana, Capuchin, Rhesus and Gibbons. Then with the addition of chipmunks, marmots, porcupines, otters, coatimundi and penguins the walled garden at last looked lived in. If the mammals were the 'furniture and fittings', then the birds were the 'décor' – eagles, owls, golden and silver pheasants and colourful parakeets and parrots. The 'ornaments' were in a new walk-through tropical aviary – touracos, bulbuls, babblers, cardinals and humming birds. The 'mobiles' were the free-flying macaws and the free-strutting peacocks.

In the parklands the flamingoes, cranes, pelicans, storks, swans, ducks, rheas and emus lived harmoniously together with llamas and wallabies, and the deer had emerged from their woodland hiding place to be replaced by beavers, which were for ever heard but not seen. Some animals had come and gone. A lion cub and a young polar bear which had been kept only for one season, a pair of tapirs, 'Roberta' and 'Toughy Snooks', and all the residents of a nocturnal house – flying foxes, armadilloes and kinkajous.

New cages and enclosures were constructed to house the new intake, and old ones were improved to provide more space and better vegetation for the animals. Some of these John designed himself, while at the same time designing buildings for other wild-life parks. Visitors were coming in ever-increasing numbers. The appeal of the estate was being broadened to attract everybody from enthusiastic naturalists, zoologists and horticulturalists to those who hated animal captivity. In addition to the obligatory loos, car parks, restaurant, first-aid posts and shelters, some other attractions had to be provided for people who were indifferent to the wild life centrepiece. A picnic area, a souvenir shop, and a garden shop provided more stopping points for people who could not keep up their interest in animals. A suprising number of the visitors were never getting beyond the walled garden in spite of an abundance of notices directing them to the paddocks and the lakes. Cricket was trying to offer a full day out for the family. While a footsore granny could sit under a cedar tree and commune with nature with her knitting, the children could be raising hell in the children's playground. For them there was now a tractor – an old farm vehicle which had taken on a new lease of life painted bright red and mounted on a tree stump; there was a tree house, a 'Lunar Walk', slides, swings, ropes and pony rides. All human life was there, and more besides, since by now two visitors had even died on the estate. As a result of these deaths a doctor seriously suggested that a mortuary would be a priority as a public facility.

But on the whole it looked as if Cricket's 'fox, chicken and bag of corn' dilemma had been solved. All the inhabitants and the visitors seemed well content. For the animals, a sure sign of contentment is breeding. Unhappy animals do not breed. The birth of young waterfowl, birds, wild cats, deer, wallabies, monkeys, llamas and camel confirmed that a satisfactory environment had been created. If this criterion applied to humans, then Rosemary, too, was content in her habitat. She, too, was breeding fast – a second child, Jeremy, born and another on the way.

Some of the animals were remarkably cooperative in contributing to the idyllic façade which the park was presenting to the public. Some of the relationships were not only cordial but deeply affectionate. It is difficult to see what a camel would have in common with a Dexter cow – a chubby black beast with short legs – and a goat. The three were originally put in the same enclosure on the assurance that no harm could come of it, but nobody could have foreseen that this grouping would blossom into an abiding love, a *ménage à trois*. There was a barnacle goose which grew up convinced it was a deer, and spent most of its adolescence apparently looking for a suitable mate among the sika. It used to follow one particular hind everywhere it went and would rub its beak tenderly against her back legs. This was love unrequited – the deer did not take much notice. A group of guinea fowl appeared to develop a crush on one of the rheas, and pursued it wherever it went. This was an illusion dispelled if one watched the stalking for long enough, when the fowls' real designs became clear. Whenever the rhea defecated they would excitedly home in on the droppings and devour them. Another strange relationship – one in which ornithologists still refuse to believe – developed in the aviaries between the spotted eagle owls and a family of ordinary hedge sparrows. The marvel was not that the owls liked the sparrows particularly, but that they did not kill them – something they would certainly do in the wild; indeed they allowed them to nest in a gooseberry bush in the middle of their aviary, and did not molest them – even when they were nesting themselves.

It was tempting to point to these tableaux of blissful harmony, and to claim that Cricket had created a Happy Valley, had appealed to its creatures' better nature, had conquered their wildest instincts, and soothed the savage beast. But it would be far from the truth. The picture of serene tranquillity which the visitors saw obscured an undercurrent of hostilities, contests and dangers which it was for the managers to keep in check. Most animals kept to themselves and out of each other's way. But occasionally one stepped out of line. Peaceful co-existence is always uneventful, but animosity manifests itself in the ugliest of scenes. One was rarely witness to these flare-ups since the animals arranged to have their struggles when nobody was looking, but the results were always plain enough.

One morning John was on his early morning rounds and found three dead wallabies – their bodies torn apart by some brutal attacker. He caught sight of the culprit slinking away along the top of the wall. It was perhaps the last animal he would have suspected of such a killing. John could not believe it was even capable of it. It was a lynx cub – only a few weeks old, small enough to wriggle through the three-inch weld-mesh on the roof of its cage, and a quarter of the size of the wallabies. 'Don't be fooled by appearances' is a maxim which the animal keepers always bear in mind but this was John's first practical lesson. That lynx was kept under close arrest until it had grown too big to get through the wires again.

Quite suddenly one spring another phantom killer started to strike. First a flamingo was killed, then two pelicans were found dead, their bodies lacerated. Then a wallaby was pulverized. The next victim was a demoiselle crane, then some ducks and more flamingoes were found butchered. It was mystifying. At first it was thought that these killings were the work of some outside marauder like a fox, but the enclosures were well sealed from foxes. This theory was dismissed when the next victim was found. Lying in the middle of the paddock with its stomach ripped open was the dead body of the pride of the park – the magnificent wapiti – whose imposing figure had for four seasons been the pin-up for the cover of the brochure. His companion was over on the other side of the enclosure: Pimple, the red deer, also bore the scars of an embittered struggle. Pimple was clearly responsible for this and possibly the other deaths as well. He had a record of violence and a reputation for viciousness, though he had previously reserved his animosity for humans, and in two seasons had never shown any hostility to other animals. He had been hand-reared and had no fear of humans; he disliked people intensely, particularly the curator. On one occasion the vet had to catch him for treatment, but could not inveigle him to the corner where the operation was to take place. Boldly the curator presented himself as a decoy. Although Pimple was stationed as far away as he could be, one look at his arch-enemy in the distance was enough to have the malicious beast charging across the paddock to do battle. But, once the curator had slipped out of the firing line, Pimple was galloping headlong into the veterinary ambush. This red deer had injured other keepers and had them on the ground several times, so it was kept well away from visitors. But why he had suddenly turned on the other animals and birds remained a mystery. Pimple was destroyed, and with him ended that wave of mystifying slaughters.

Accidents, incidents, battles and imbalances of nature are inevitable in a wild-life park, and one can only guard against them up to a point. If the aim is to simulate a natural environment, then these are among its most natural features. The wild is far crueller than life in an animal reserve. The deer become tetchy in the rutting season, just as any animal is at its most aggressive and defensive in its breeding and rearing seasons. Even in the aviaries, where life seems at its most tranquil, quarrels and fierce skirmishes break out from time to time. When some of the birds are nesting, Alan, the birds' keeper, has to take a net into the cages with him – a danger signal they come to respect – in order to ward off their attacks. A pair of jay thrushes, transferred to a well-planted aviary to breed, once set about a magpie and killed it. A whistling thrush – put into the tropical aviary where the waterfall might provide a suitable breeding ground – began to settle down well, but suddenly pecked its mate to death and unaccountably ran amok, slaughtering twenty other birds as well. Sometimes the fights are just a struggle for dominance. The two fish eagles, both males, have tussles from time to time, the one which was there first being determined to remind the other who is boss. The scimitar babblers tried to establish their dominance over the tropical aviary more forcibly. After a period of peace they started colluding in a series of wilful murders, choosing their moments and pouncing on their waxbill victims from opposite ends of the aviary.

Even with the most expert knowledge it is not possible

to be certain which animals or birds can safely be put together. At Cricket it was often a matter of trial and error,
the trial period demanding close and constant surveillance.
More often than not, the creatures take to their new habitats,
routines and companions without protest or signs of resent-
ment. They settle down and cohabit contentedly, but
sometimes after long periods of peace – even years – there
is some upheaval which confounds even the people who
know the animals best. Although relationships appear to be
friendly, tensions are bound to occur. Inhibiting emotions
is not part of an animal's social conditioning, and squabbles
– as in even the closest family – are likely to come to the
boil. It was in such a 'family quarrel' that Fariq the camel
and his paddock mate, the zebra, eventually came to blows.
It will never be known whether Fariq really intended to
kill the zebra, but the nip he gave him pierced a crucial
blood vessel in the back of his neck and the zebra died.
This was the third of the park's zebras to die, three exceptions to the rule of good settlement and adaption. The
first – the one which jumped into the lake when it arrived –
had been let out too early one spring and succumbed to a
rare virus with the exotic name of salmonella Stanley-Cairo,
brought on by stress. Two more were ordered from the
animal dealers, and had to be imported. They arrived in
the middle of a dock strike at Hull, a stoppage which led
to one of the most explosive telephone conversations Cricket
had ever heard.

'You can't just leave them there,' John thundered when
the Hull harbourmaster had explained that his men were
refusing to load the crates on to the waiting lorry for the
final leg of their journey. John felt very helpless so far from
the docks.

'It's all we can do,' said the harbourmaster, as if it was
his final word.

'In that case the zebras will die – and you'll be responsible'.

The zebras had already been dangerously delayed and
any more hold-ups would mean certain death.

'Look,' John threatened after more argument, 'if those zebras are not on that lorry within half an hour you'll be letting them die, and I shall see that they do so in front of every pressman and television camera that I can muster.'

Within that half hour the two zebras were on their way to Cricket. The harbourmaster and a few office staff had loaded them on to the lorry themselves. But even so one of the zebras died on the journey.

Once an animal was successfully transported, providing the best natural environment was only one factor contributing to its survival. The other – an unnatural element – was human intervention. The responsibility for their feeding and welfare fell to a succession of dedicated keepers, Brian, another John, Peter, Alan, Keith, Julian, Mike, passionately devoted to their charges, and ever pandering to their whims and foibles. The job involved day and night vigilance, and in a sense the keepers themselves were in captivity. They could seldom leave the estate; it was not a question of 'taking work home' – work was home. If they left the park, work sometimes had to go too, as in the case of one keeper who had to take a puma cub he was rearing to a far-off family funeral. While the emotional and psychological well-being of the animals depended on the keepers, their physical condition and health was in the hands of a resourceful partnership of vets – ordinary country vets – who responded enthusiastically to the demands of the wilder creatures. One of them particularly, Tony Parsons, took a liking to his new patients. He was an ornithologist, already well versed in the ways and needs of tropical birds, and regarded his dealings with other exotic creatures as a natural progression. He mugged up the subject omnivorously and made contact with the country's zoological experts to qualify himself to take on the bulk of the routine and emergency treatment and surgery.

All requirements for quarantining, immunization, parasite control and inspection had to be rigorously fulfilled, and many additional precautions had to be taken to prevent disease. An outbreak of rabies, anthrax or foot-and-mouth could virtually bankrupt the whole operation in a matter of days. One has only to look at the human world to see that no amount of care, attention and medical know-how can guarantee that infections will not take root and spread, and that possibility was just as threatening in this animal microcosm. Cricket has had its share of disease and epidemics. The worst of these was an outbreak of an infection – a form of pseudo-tuberculosis – as a result of which the whole aviary had to be closed down. The same fate befell the nocturnal house, where some bushbabies, flying foxes and kinkajous succumbed to an infection and died; it was never reopened. The armadilloes brought with them the seeds of their own destruction. They lived contentedly enough for three years and then mysteriously died within several weeks of each other. The post-mortem – a baffling inquiry in which the remains were analysed by Bristol University and the London School of Tropical Medicine – showed that all three were possessed of an obscure parasite which had been first classified in 1912 and had never been heard of since.

Food poisoning was another ever-present threat, but Cricket managed to avoid much of this risk by feeding the carnivores fresh meat killed on the estate itself. One or two monkeys had died of enteritis as a result of something they had eaten, and in another case a gibbon died after being given a lollipop by a visitor who, presumably, could not read the 'Do not Feed' notices. Perhaps the oddest postmortem that Tony Parsons had ever had to conduct was on one of the rheas which suddenly dropped dead in its paddock. In its stomach he found a carved doll's head which looked as if it could have been made by South American Indians. He could only speculate how long it had been there, since this creature came from the South American wild itself. The import of this work of art must rate as one of the most original smuggling ideas ever conceived. Tony also extracted five old pennies and a half-crown which had long ceased to be legal tender. Although the bird died of avian pasteurellosis, he was tempted to put 'Decimaliza-tion' or 'Inflation' as cause of death.

Tony's transition from domestic to wild animals was not too difficult, but it meant learning some new skills. One of these was using a dog-catcher – an unwieldy implement consisting of a steel tube with a looped length of wire through it, a sort of metal lasso. Before the park owned a dart gun which could anaesthetize surgery cases from a distance, the dog-catcher was used to collar the wilder animals from outside the cages and haul them to the bars for their injections. This had almost invariably been the most agonizing stage of any of the operations he had had to perform, and on one occasion, a civet cat, about to be treated for sore paws, tried to bite through the steel tube with such vehemence that it broke off several of its front teeth.

With over a thousand animals on his panel, he has to be prepared for almost anything – from oiling an elephant to delivering a leopard cub by Caesarian section. One corner of the zoo kitchens was set aside as a hospital where the various pills and medicines were kept. This is where the operations on the smaller animals are done, but if the patient is a camel with a broken leg, or a llama in labour, the operation must be done *in situ*. The hospital also acts as winter quarters for some of the animals and birds which do not like the cold weather. Among these is one of the vultures which is susceptible to frostbite and which had already lost two of its toes before it came to Cricket. Another 'factory reject' was a gibbon which only had one hand. Placed alongside a diana monkey convalescing after having its injured tail removed, these dismembered exhibits cer-tainly gave the place the look of a casualty department. What was more, they were still on display and the visitors could look in on them from the public footways. The spectacle led one visitor to the conclusion that the whole park was a home for sick animals. One could not accuse any of the patients of 'malingering' – except perhaps the herons. These are technically not the park's responsibility and fly in from all over Somerset, ostensibly in search of medical attention. They seem to have heard of Tony's avian National Health Service and arrive with all manner of broken bones and other disorders, confident that once they touch down they automatically join his panel. It is a curious phenomenon, Cricket's answer to the 'Flying Doctor' – the 'Flying Patient'. Tony can only oblige them, after which some fly off and others settle down in the park, often presenting bird spotters with identification problems; if they needed surgery they will have been sprayed with an antibiotic – a deep purple liquid which stains their feathers for a time. A heron-like bird with purple streaks is an extremely rare specimen.

The toll of death, casualty and sickness has been remarkably light considering the number and variety of animals living at such close quarters. Experienced zoologists and animal experts who may at first have considered the Cricket venture as a faltering, inept, and unqualified attempt to run a safari park were by this time looking at it differently. Soon Cricket was listed as 'very good' in a nation-wide university survey of animal reserves. Ninety-nine per cent of the animals adapt, live and breed without needing any special attention and can boast that they have never lost a day's work due to ill-health. 'Work' to them was just being there, and making themselves conspicuous and amenable to visitors. It was a function they were fulfilling admirably, and the visitors seemed satisfied enough. In fact, their opinions, which had been low-key in the early seasons, were now becoming quite laudatory. The managers always made a point of mingling incognito with the crowds from time to time to gauge public opinion.

'Hello,' said Paddy to a man in a tartan hat he felt he ought to know but could not place. 'You here again?' It was a safe opening gambit.

'See you've got our elephant then.'

'*Your* elephant?'

'Last year the wife wrote saying you should get another elephant. Company for the other one, like.'

'We aim to please,' said Paddy humbly.

'And the year before that my lad here wanted to see a camel and then you get a camel.'

'Perhaps you'd like to put in your order for next year,' Paddy suggested.

'Walruses,' said a nine-year-old.

It had become the policy to make a significant addition to the animal collection each year, and to add as many new attractions as possible so that visitors would keep coming back year after year. When the season closes in October it is time to consider what changes might be made for the following March. Here was a positive suggestion. Walruses. Wild-like parks like other businesses are subject to the laws of supply and demand, and walruses were in short supply. But sealions were plentiful. John ordered three sealions to top the bill of the following season's new attractions.

Each winter is spent building new enclosures, patching up old ones and overhauling the estate after the ravages of a quarter of a million people and thousands of cars. For the animals it may mean a certain amount of upheaval and being shifted about. Some of them may have to leave the estate altogether to be taken to other parks, and new ones are brought in in the spring. As transportation is perhaps the most unpleasant ordeal which a zoo animal has to endure, John liked where possible to collect and deliver the Cricket animals himself to ensure minimum discomfort. The sealions were among his passengers on perhaps the most nerve racking of these periodic hauls.

John had hired a truck to collect some leopards, monkeys and deer from Yorkshire and to return via Nuneaton to pick up the sealions. It was a twenty-four-hour round trip, so he took his sister Jill to share the driving, and a mattress, sleeping bags and blankets so that neither need lose any sleep on the journey. On the way back John had driven most of the night and was feeling tired, so he handed over to Jill, and clambered into the back of the truck where his bed was laid out on top of the animal crates. Soon he was sound asleep. But the monkeys were wide awake, and kept reaching through the sliding door into the cab and pulling Jill's hair. When this became too irritating she slammed the door shut. After a few hours of motorway driving Jill was hungry and wanted to stop for breakfast. Soon she was driving up a service road towards a motorway café, and began changing down at the top of the incline. But something went wrong with her gear changing as she entered the car park; her foot missed the accelerator and hit the brake and the truck halted far less gracefully than she had intended. In the formidable lurch, John suddenly found himself hurled off the top of the crates and plummeting to the floor between them, where he was entombed in an avalanche of bedding. He woke up to find himself upside down in the dark, pinioned in his sleeping bag and wedged between two crates, a leopard breathing in his face on one side and monkeys pulling his hair on the other.

'Sorry,' Jill shouted through the closed door, her voice drowned by the vibrations of shifting crates and the chorus of animal protests.

'What do you think you're doing?' came John's muffled voice through his layer of blankets.

'Having breakfast. Coming?'

'Help – I'm stuck. Open this door.'

Jill gripped the door handle and pulled. It would not move.

'It's jammed. Something must be up against it. Can you shift it?'

'No, push harder.'

It was when Jill inched the door open that John realized what was jamming it. A stabbing pain told him that it was his own foot. A bit of wriggling freed it and the door slid open, to admit an inhabited sleeping bag which caterpillared backwards into the cab followed by a very red face.

'Good morning,' said John casually. 'Houdini's the name.'

'Houdini' would have been a much better name for one of those sealions – the great escaper. But little did John know then of the sealion adventures which lay in store. Nor did he know that they were soon to announce their arrival at Cricket somewhat flamboyantly. While he had been away the lakes were being made sealion-worthy. They had been drained and cleaned, but when the new residents arrived, they had only just started to fill up again. The problem was where to put the sealions in the meantime – the bath? a cattle trough? the ornamental pond? Just outside the house is a magnificent fountain – mock-Greek with an ample well ten feet across with a fulsome spray of water sprouting from a stone cornucopia.

'Turn it on – fill it up,' said John, cordoning off an area of lawn round the fountain with a roll of wire netting. 'They can go in here.'

'Yaaaggghhhhh,' the sealions barked as they slithered into the water. It was an ear-splitting sound which was to become the dominant sound of the park. Their stentorian bark could be heard from half a mile away and sounded like the strangled cry of a basso-profundo being thrown over a cliff by the throat. It was late in the evening. Paddy had been on the farms all day and no one had told him that any sealions had arrived – even less that they were parked right underneath his bedroom window. As he went to bed, he turned on the radio for the weather forecast. 'It will remain dry throughout the south-west, temperature reaching seventy in most areas.' He switched off, only to become aware of a new sound – water sheeting against the window-panes.

'What are they talking about – can't they see it's pouring with rain!'

His mumbling was interrupted by another sound. A piercing shriek.

'Yaaaarrrrghhh!'

'What the devil's that!' he spluttered, bounding across the room and throwing up the window to admit a spray of water, which soaked his pyjamas. He peered out into the darkness.

'Who's that? Are you all right?'

Doreen was coming into the bedroom behind him as he sized up half the situation.

'Oh – I see, it's the fountain. But who's that fool lying in the grass?'

'It's a sealion – there are three of them,' explained Doreen.

'Bless me, so there are. Nobody tells me anything.'

'Yaaaarrrggghhhh.'

'Have we got to put up with that racket all night?'

'John says they'll settle down.'

Paddy bid them good night with a cheery 'Shut up and let a man get some sleep', slammed the window down and changed into some dry pyjamas. John had been wrong. The sealions in the fountain kept up their barking all night, as each tired, another taking up the chorus.

'Yarrgghhhh, yaaarrrrrghhh, Yaaaarrrghhhhh.'

Roughly translated, 'It wasn't like this in Nuneaton.'

6

We're Here'

When you have several thousand animals in your 'family' it is impossible to establish personal relations with all of them. Only a small proportion are dependent on human company and even less show any personal response. The borderline separating those which do from those which do not is crossed once the animal has a name. Twiggy, Tom, Zanda, Fariq, Pimple, Merlin, Bert, Gert and Daisy, and Chikki, once christened, are admitted into what the sociologists call the 'nuclear family'; the rest are cousins, anything from once to several times removed.

Choosing a name is done in several ways. Some, like Tom – the leopard which became the mascot of Cricket St Thomas – had a certain logic about them, while others like Pimple – the intolerable red deer – remain a mystery. Twiggy seems a plausible name for an elephant by virtue of its sheer absurdity, but Fariq has an appropriate Eastern flavour about it, although this particular camel was born and bred in Yorkshire, and is right proud of it. The names Merlin for an owl, or Foot-tapper for a macaw, denote something of their personality or habits, but some animals defy descriptive names. Chikki for the baby elephant and Lyra for a lynx cub were chosen from hundreds of suggestions sent in for a competition in a local newspaper. Others like Tish, Myra, Gonk and Toughy Snooks are just handles – names for want of better ones. Some residents do not need names. What is the point of calling a flamingo anything when it is one of fifty and completely indistinguishable from the others, and unlikely to come when it is called, even if there was any need to call it? Besides, what do you call a flamingo? They stand on one leg, so Long John or Ahab would be obvious choices, but you run out of uniped names long before the flock is dubbed. So unless they rise above the general level of ordinary life, or distinguish themselves and make their presence felt in some way, the animals remain anonymous.

It is impossible not to have favourites among the animals, and they are the ones which have stamped their own mark on the life of the park, or imposed their own personalities in such a way as to win the special esteem of both staff and visitors.

To find favour with the visitors, it helps the animals to have one of several genetic advantages. One is to have what the image-builders call 'presence' – the elephants, camel, leopards, and eagles have this natural charisma. Another is to have beauty, as do peacocks, flamingoes and the other most colourful birds. But perhaps more than these what people enjoy in an animal are human characteristics, because these enable them to communicate – or think they can. Hence they like the monkeys. They like raccoons too, since they have the human trait of washing their food before meals which they eat hand-to-mouth sitting up at their places with impeccable table manners. They like the mynah birds, parrots and macaws because they talk. If the point needs proving one only has to hear the gales of public delight which greet the keepers when they appear in a cage in the absence of, say, the pumas, and start mucking out behind a notice saying 'This animal is Dangerous'. The other factor the visitors look for is cuddliness, which accounts for the popularity of the pets' corner, full of rabbits, guinea-pigs and lambs.

But the animals do not rely on these outward appearances and displays to endear themselves to or impress themselves on the keepers. The keepers know them better and like or dislike them for their personalities. Their closer contact and observation reveal that most of their charges are rich in character, and show not only traits which are characteristic of their kind but also tendencies and foibles which mark them out as individuals. One would expect elephants and monkeys to have personalities of their own, but one does not look for individualism in say porcupines or penguins. Yet even Cricket's porcupine, for instance, is quite a character, if not a particularly pleasant one. He is an aggressive creature and does not much care for visitors. He is a comical figure with no sense of humour and if people laugh at him he stamps one of his back feet in exasperation. The penguins which live in the next pit look rather gormless and idle, but these are particularly industrious birds. They secretly busy themselves with the task of moving a pile of stones from one corner of the compound to the other and back again, and behave as if they do not want the keepers to know that they are doing it. One expects beauty in birds, not character, but an encounter with Cricket's rascal macaws for instance would indicate that they can have both. Foot-tapper – so called because of his nervous drubbing on his perch – says 'Hello' and a few other pleasantries, but relies on more demonstrative ways of expressing himself. He develops personal dislikes for certain people – always women – and dives down out of the sky at them like a Kamikazi pilot and does some hit-and-run clawing and pecking. One of his sworn enemies was a girl who worked at the café who used to park her bike around the back. At knocking-off time, Foot-tapper would be waiting for her, and his attacks became so predictable that somebody else always had to get her bike for her, so that she could make a speedy getaway. Foot-tapper's mate, Gonk, is more placid but her language is deplorable and she has an indelicate way of telling people to go away in as many words, but not the same ones (she was tutored in obscenity by one of the keepers just before he left). Gonk has a way of flying up into the trees and refusing to come down again. Her longest stay in the tree-tops was five days and every effort to get her down having failed, Alan, the bird keeper, had to phone for the fire brigade. By the time he was back at the tree Gonk had thought better of it and flown down, and the emergency call was cancelled. Another macaw, Rupert, never grew up and was always nervous and frightened. If the other macaws flew off on some expedition, Rupert would fly to wherever Alan happened to be in search of consolation and protection.

Who would have thought that a vulture could be a friendly cuddly creature? Chuffers, like all vultures, is not well-endowed with beauty but he makes up for it with an affable nature and he really appreciates any affection shown him, after all he gets little enough of it. 'Yuk,' say the visitors and bustle on without a thought for Chuffer's constatly waning morale. Only Alan can restore his ego, which he does by tickling the vulture's head, much to the astonishment of visitors. They admire his daring in going into the cage at all. 'I've left him my body when I die,' is Alan's usual crack, which always get a weak laugh. Other characters in the aviaries include Sundance, a Reeves pheasant, which over the months has pecked its way through six pairs of Alan's boots; a woodpecker which is systematically demolishing the cage woodwork and an aristocratic grey hornbill which considers itself superior to the other occupants of its aviaries and their mundane preoccupations. It dines alone.

Most of the animals develop a special attachment to one or other of the keepers, usually a fair return for the amount of special interest and care the keepers take. It is unusual for any animal to ride equally high in the esteem of all the keepers and of estate people and visitors. Cricket has known three notable exceptions: Twiggy and Chikki, the elephants, and Tom, the leopard.

Twiggy and Chikki have deserved every atom of tender loving care, expense, time, and affection which has been lavished on them. Periodic lapses into mischief, falls from grace, and even downright naughtiness have not eroded the reserves of goodwill they have stored up. However, Tom – the leopard cub – who started life in everybody's good books, eventually overplayed his hand.

It was not that Tom was in any way different from other

leopards, but that he had been brought up differently. More than any other animal at Cricket he was raised in a human world, the manner of his upbringing not being intentional or experimental, but a matter of survival. It was the inevitable result of his dramatic arrival. The circumstances of his unusual birth can be traced to the previous year when Tish, the mother leopard, had last had a cub. On that occasion her keeper noticed that she was having difficulty with the birth and called the vet, who arrived just as the cub was emerging. It was obvious that the pelvic cavity was too small to allow the cub to pass through, and the survival of the mother and cub now depended on human intervention. Interceding at this late stage of delivery was no easy matter, but it was fortunately the first resort which had to require results. Probing through the cage well-mesh with the dog-catcher, the vet managed to get a grip on the cub, and Tish finished the job by walking away. But the cub was dead. The tragedy sounded a cautionary note for the next time Tish went into labour, when they could expect a Caesarian operation to be necessary.

This occurred one May afternoon, and Tony, the vet, was there in good time. Cursory inspection revealed that Tish was again in difficulties. The park did not have a dart gun at this time, but as Tish was sitting at the edge of her cage it was easy to get the first tranquillizing injection into her tail. The drug took a long time to pass through the creature and there was a half-hour's hiatus before she was sufficiently docile to be approached from inside the cage. Even then she could not be trusted, so administering the full anaesthetic was a four-man job. One held her with the dog catcher through the bars, and Tony and the two others went inside the cage and approached her, pushing before them a tea chest with its two sides cut away. Enveloping her with the tea chest, they forced her to the edge of the cage where Tony cut a hole in the plywood through which he could implant his hypodermic. There was no time now to take the anaesthetized leopard to the surgery; she was carried up to the Big House on a food trolley and laid out on Rosemary's kitchen table.

To say that the operation went smoothly would not tell the full story. For Tony it was a routine operation, though it was his first leopard Caesarian, and certainly the first major surgery he had performed with a family hovering round him, drinking cups of tea, taking photographs, a mother trying to make cakes, grandmother trying to hustle the children out of the room, and a baby in a high chair bawling for its supper. Yet he was successful. First one cub emerged, but it was dead, and then came Tom – more dead than alive. Tony handed over the wet yellow rat-like creature to John to sponge clean. Its breathing was staccato and lethargic. Some of this inertia was due to the drugs which would by now have been transmitted to the cub from the mother, and it was now for John to massage it, and to give it the kiss of life, which he did through a child's 'whirly' drinking straw.

As he nursed the cub, John kept half an eye on the mother which Tony was now stitching up.

Suddenly to his horror he saw the leopard begin to come to life with a slow stretching movement of the front and back paw, then a slight twitch of the head. An awesome prospect for which he had made no provisions at once took on a stark reality. What if the mother came round now and ran amok round the kitchen with an open wound in her stomach with everybody there and the children . . . ? All the stories of enraged wounded beasts in the wild and their ferocity came to mind. He looked at Tony, who was pre-occupied with his stitching and did not appear to have noticed Tish's signs of revival. Suddenly she let out a growl, swung her paws in the air, and began to roll over wriggling.

'Oh no,' groaned John, leaping up and bracing himself for an ugly scene.

But the alarm was unnecessary. Tish finished her convulsion and sank back into oblivion.

'That's quite common,' said Tony coolly. 'It's the mix of the drugs. I knew I'd given her a big enough dose.'

Tish slept on for another twenty-four hours, which proved his point.

Keeping Tom alive was touch and go for the next few hours. His survival hereafter was a human responsibility. After her experience of the Caesarian the mother would not accept him, and would probably have killed him if he were put in her cage. He therefore had to be nursed day and night – a full-time job for somebody. It fell to John. Every two hours thereafter he had to go to the box by the kitchen stove, lift the cub out and persuade him to take milk from a syringe. The rest of the time Tom slept.

Tom's progress was steady, and no doubt he gained strength from the moral support he was getting from everybody on the estate. He was now the centre of attention, and won the celebrity of a new baby. Each new movement or sign of progress was noted and broadcast and every feed and bowel movement became a topic of discussion. It was the latter which gave John his first cause for alarm, for while Tom was putting away his milk voraciously, nothing seemed to be coming out the other end and there was obviously a limit to the length of time this state of affairs could harmlessly continue. When that limit was reached and crossed – nearly a week after he was born – Tom's future looked in jeopardy. He either had an anatomical blockage of some sort or he was severely constipated.

'Liquid paraffin,' suggested Doreen. 'That should get him going.'

'Spinach and figs, that's what does for me,' Paddy disclosed.

'Well, he's not you, is he. He's a leopard,' John reminded him.

'I could liquidize some prunes,' said Rosemary.

'I know! I've got just the thing!' exclaimed Doreen and skipped out of the room. In a few moments she was back cradling a little soap suppository in her hands.

'I've warmed it,' she explained, handing the minute torpedo to John.

It worked. Within minutes Tom had performed his first

creative act, the product welcomed in the household as ecstatically as the Queen of Sheba in the court of King Solomon.

Tom's health was never again a problem or even a matter for speculation. He grew well, fed willingly, and slept and played. The maternal responsibilities for his ablutions were taken over by Fawn the whippet, who was summoned at the end of every feed and presented with Tom's lumbar regions to lick. Otherwise the cub's only contact with other animals was with the two baby fawns which were also being reared in the house. This was a particularly good summer for the children. Tom proved a sporting playmate, a sucker for rough and tumble. Celia and Jeremy used to play with him in the garden, and Olivia, Rosemary's third child, would invite him into her pram and insist on his sharing her bottle. To the children there was nothing strange about having such an exotic pet. Celia was as old as the park itself, and neither she nor the younger ones had known anything but an animal-orientated life. Their contribution to the park operation was to pose with the animals for press and publicity photographs. Olivia was only slightly older than Tom, and together they made an attractive pair, and pictures of them sharing a pram or squabbling for the possession of toys cropped up from time to time in papers, magazines, or on television. But Tom grew up faster than Olivia and when he became too boisterous for her, their cradle companionship came to an end. When he was quite tiny, Tom used to romp about with his claws out, but when he discovered what they were for he put them away until they were needed. Sometimes the older children would tease him and then run away, and he would chase them. This was a good game, until they found that Tom was catching them up and clawing their legs. The tables were turned and the children became wary of him. So did Woolworths – an in-law retriever puppy, who suddenly found Tom was getting the upper paw. Up to this time Tom slept in his box by the stove and spent the day padding about the house. When the stove ran out of fuel one day he was moved to another warm spot – the office safe; here he guarded the takings, coming out from time to time to go through the wastepaper baskets and chew the telephone cables. He became the park's mascot, and was proudly shown to visitors and brought to board meetings and parties. John took him out for walks on a lead several times a day when he was always the centre of attention though some of the other animals did not much care for him.

When he was brought into the walled garden a cacophony of animal voices passed a warning from cage to cage; some of the monkeys would go indoors and even the lynx would arch their backs and slink into a protected corner of their enclosure, while some of the rodents would scurry about in their pens with evident alarm. Taking a leopard for a walk is not the same thing as taking a dog out. For a cat, locomotion has no merits in itself. A dog can be trained to trot along beside its handler at a steady pace, but Tom could see no sense in that. He made headway in leaps and bounds, determined by what there was to bound at and what points of interest needed investigating. This made the walks difficult for John, particularly when he was himself out on his business rounds and was trying to talk to the men. It was common for him suddenly to be dragged off in mid-sentence. He was once seen to vanish through a flower-bed and another time to go clean over a wall.

It was soon, however, becoming obvious that Tom was becoming too difficult to handle and too dangerous to be regarded as a domestic animal. The playful nips and scratches which he had inflicted on John, Paddy, the keepers, and others who had at some time had to look after him, were now being superseded by more severe wounds. It is difficult to know exactly when a wild animal ceases to be a pet and actually becomes a hazard, and when security and companionship become incompatible. But between the two points there is a period in which the animal starts posing a threat but does not actually commit any offence sufficiently reprehensible to justify his being locked up. Tom was moved out of the house and into a cage by the dog kennels, but he continued to go for walks with anyone he knew and cared to take him, and provided he was on the lead he could be kept under control. However, he was very quickly growing into a fearsome-looking beast and his teeth were awe-inspiring even when he was only smiling. One afternoon someone was wandering with Tom on the lead through the drawing room, where the piano tuner was tinkering under the lid of the piano. Tom saw him and sprang into the instrument with him. The piano tuner went completely white and needed much consoling. That piano needed tuning again in two weeks, so he probably left without tightening the strings.

Even so, this encounter was probably not so traumatic as that experienced by a woman who, just before closing time one summer night, decided to go to the Ladies'. John thought all the cubicles were empty and went in to investigate a leak in the plumbing taking Tom in with him. The sound of male voices in a Ladies' is enough to alarm any self-respecting female, but it also presents the possibility that she might have found her way into the Gents'. Whichever it was, she decided to sit tight until the danger had passed and she could emerge unmolested. John, not knowing she was there, was quite happily talking to Tom, whom the incarcerated woman took to be a rather silent and asthmatic plumber's mate. Having mended the errant ballcock, John was leading Tom down the line of cubicles when Tom suddenly slipped underneath the one closed door. It is hard to imagine a more terrifying experience that to be sitting on the loo and suddenly to have a leopard crawling under the door and snarling at you. This is the story that lady will tell her grandchildren, ending, 'but it wasn't funny at the time'. Nor could it have been. She was not to know that Tom was on the lead and that John had him quite under control. She let out a piercing scream and jumped on to the seat, a reaction which scared both John and Tom right out of the Ladies'. It was some time before she could be coaxed out, but in one sense for a scare of this scale it was a good thing it happened where it did.

Even in the park, where one would expect to see a leopard, Tom was something of a novelty, and naturally the further away from Cricket he got, the more his presence became a source of amazement to people. Londoners, particularly, found him intriguing, and one visit was enough to disprove the theory that one can do anything in London and no one will turn a hair. Walk a leopard up the King's Road and you will see many an eyelid being batted. Not only that, but people are moved to do extraordinary things, their reaction ranging from fascination to outraged indignation.

Tom's first appearance in Battersea Park for an early-morning constitutional had elderly matrons running hysterically in all directions scooping up their pekes and poodles, while other regulars stood their ground and churlishly snarled something like 'Fancy bringing that thing in here'. On the other hand, some people, assuming that the presence of a handler and a lead meant that Tom was tame, wanted to put their heads in his mouth. But it takes more than a leopard to excite the sanguine London taxi-driver. When Tom took his first taxi ride the cabby's only concern was for the preservation of his upholstery, and, saying something to that effect, he accepted the fare like any other, slamming the glass partition tightly shut, and spending the journey wondering what extras he was entitled to extort for leopards. A top-hatted hotel doorman who met the taxi must have assumed at first glance that Tom was either the upholstery or a befurred dowager reclining in it, and was somewhat startled on opening the door when the lady on the seat leapt into his arms.

Reactions are many and varied, but, after a little experience, predictable. If someone sees John with Tom a long way off, the distance will enable the beholder to make the appropriate psychological adjustment, but if they see that formidable face suddenly at close quarters the shock will have them instinctively recoiling and then rebounding with all manner of abuse and vilification. But no one is more scared or on tenterhooks during Tom's public appearances than John himself, ever mindful not only of what he does –

like pee and chew things – which are socially embarrassing, but also of what he might do – like dismember or kill people, which would also constitute a breach of protocol.

It will never be known what Mrs Beeton would have had to say about the correct etiquette for leopards at weddings, but one can be sure that romping on the floor with the bridegroom, peeing on the carpet, and eating the hems of ladies' dresses would be fairly low in the prescribed code of conduct. This particular society wedding involved a model who was a little concerned that in the absence of some gimmick the event might not get into the papers. Tom was invited to be the gimmick and John, aware of the publicity value to the park, was prepared to accompany him.

The occasion began in a swish Knightsbridge flat overlooking Harrods, where the wedding party was assembling, where Tom immediately diverted all the attention – rightly the bride's – towards himself with a minor indiscretion on the Wilton. He was then given champagne, which he sniffed and sneezed out of its saucer. He declined a salmon sandwich more politely and started looking around for carcasses-on-sticks, of which there were none to be found. Many a dog would have had its nose rapped for foraging around in the trays of canapés in the way Tom was allowed to, the normal rules waived in deference to who would have the last word if it came to an argument. As people became more and more familiar with Tom, who was lulling them into a false sense of security, that possibility loomed larger and larger until John's instinct warned him to call the games off.

A lift must be one of the worst places to experience one's first encounter with a leopard. John knew that however tightly reined Tom was, any fellow occupant of a lift was within range, and had hung back from the main body of the descending wedding party to get a lift to himself. But, as luck would have it, the lift stopped one floor down to admit an elegant young female in a long dress who was well inside the closing doors before Tom revealed himself from behind John's legs. There is something about a lift which brings out the phlegmatic side of the British character – as if Mrs

Beeton had laid down that the correct form was to rein one-self in, hold one's breath and stand rigidly staring aloft at the flashing floor numbers in pious silence. The girl saw Tom and without a hint of alarm or incredulity pressed the button for the next floor, although her empty shopping bags denoted an original intention to go the whole way. As the doors opened and the girl was bringing off her composed exit, Tom gently stretched out a claw and extracted a strand of thread from the hem of her dress, thereby starting a cascade of unstitching which continued as she walked away. The doors closed on a length of green thread and the lift descended – no doubt leaving the girl with a mini-dress before she got to the bottom of the stairs and a G-string before she was out of the building.

If Tom had been looking for a chance to cause maximum disruption, he could not have chosen his moment more shrewdly. After the registry-office ceremony the wedding group was posing in the King's Road for the photographs. For Tom this was the purpose of the whole exercise. The picture was to be of the bride, with the groom holding Tom, surrounded by the family – a cast for which John did not qualify. Yet he could not relinquish his responsibility for Tom, so he crouched down behind the bride's dress and whispered soothing words through a forest of legs. As the photographer was about to press the button, Tom began to edge backwards into the group and although the groom was gripping the lead tightly, he slipped his collar and ran back into the building hotly pursued by John. The shutter clicked. Somewhere in that wedding album is a photograph of blurred in-laws being bowled over by John's lurch at the fugitive animal, providing a hazy background for a smiling bride, arm-in-arm with a groom holding a lead and an empty collar – a symbolic omen for a marriage if ever there was one.

By any standards Tom was becoming a celebrity. He had made several regional television appearances, and was soon booked for Johnny Morris's 'Animal Magic' and 'Blue Peter' which meant another trip to London. The idea for the 'Blue Peter' programme was to introduce him to a possible mate, a female cub from the Cotswold Wild Life Park. It was a blind date, and when the two animals arrived the production team were alarmed to find that Tom was twice as old and three times the size of his 'intended'. He was also considerably more boisterous, a fact which caused Valerie Singleton, who was to preside over this televised introduction, to send a taxi home to fetch a more riskable dress than the one she was intending to wear.

As it happened the programme proved more interesting for Tom than the run-of-the-mill 'Lie-still-and-be-talked-about' appearances he'd been used to. The other items on the same show were a Uri Geller fork-bending pre-recording, and a demonstration of a new gymnasium team game. The first had been recorded that morning, and the tray of forks was melting on a desk in the corner of the studio, but the camera rehearsal for the gymnastics was in full swing when Tom arrived. The game involved two teams of leggy youths running round in circles bouncing a ball against a tilted trampoline in the hope that an opponent would drop it on the rebound. Needless to say, it bounced out of the playing area several times. This was more than Tom could have wished for. Every time it came out of bounds Tom was after it, heaving John after him and dragging him across the well-waxed studio floor. After a few tables had been overturned and the floor was littered with bent forks, Tom was put back in his crate to cool down, for fear – as much as anything – that Geller's famous delayed action psychic ether might melt Tom's collar clip, or, worse, the bars of his crate. Thereafter Tom decided not to cooperate with the programme, which was live. On a nod from the floor-manager, John was to lead Tom on his 'walk-down' from the wings to the plinth where the 'Blue Peter' interviewing panel had taken up their positions, but leaving a wider berth for their guest than usual. When the cue came, Tom stepped on to the slippery floor surface and fell over. John, being more of a showman, was striding all smiles towards his inquisitors, and because Tom was sliding so easily across the floor was not at once aware that he was not on his feet. Sensing an element of resistance, he stopped, but all his efforts to restore the animal's equilibrium were wasted, with the result that he had to carry him the rest of the way. Not one of the great entries. Nor did either of the two leopards take a blind bit of notice of each other from beginning to end, although the script was insisting that they were already passionately infatuated. Tom remained head over heels, but not in love.

Tom made several other public appearances. As a television celebrity, he opened a fête or two, was guest of honour at the opening of a catering exhibition, and, later in the year, officiated as chief balloon-popper at a kid's Christmas party. This was at the nearby naval base, and was a party which was to begin Tom's long and happy association with the navy. Soon he was to have letters after his name: 'Thomas R N'.

John was talking about Tom one day to a hunting acquaintance, a retired navy admiral who began to recall his own experience of leopards. This amounted to his service on H M S *Leopard*, when a cub rather like Tom had been the ship's mascot. This, John thought, might be just the career for Tom.

Firing off an exploratory letter addressed 'H M Ships, London' John inquired whether an H M S *Leopard* was still in service and, if so, were there any mascotting vacancies? To his surprise the reply came that there was indeed an H M S *Leopard*, and although the previous mascot had died, the post had not yet been filled and would Tom be interested in the appointment?

His last public appearance, therefore, as anything other than a zoo exhibit was on board H M S *Leopard*, moored in Portsmouth harbour alongside H M S *Victory*, which reminded John that *Leopard* was only the second ship to establish tenuous connections with Cricket. Tom's official induction looks more ceremonious in the records than it was in the event. The photographs of him posing sedately with the top brass suggest that he rose to the occasion and behaved. But in between photographs he was just as much of a handful as ever, finding quarterdeck and companionway paintwork just as amenable as carpets and curtains for his usual stock of vandalism and indiscretion.

The ship's insignia, formally presented to John, now hangs on the bars of Tom's cage, though Tom himself is no longer in it. The final chapter of his early life is not for the squeamish. Early one Sunday morning, John took him for his early-morning walk, leaving his cage door open. That cage was situated apart from the walled garden with the others and was nearer the house. While they were out, Roulette, the family's old Jack Russell terrier, strolled into the cage and concealed herself in his shelter at the back where Tom's leftovers included succulent morsels. When Tom returned to the cage he was on to the little dog before John could realize that she was there. He killed her instantly. It was a tragic end to that faithful dog, who throughout her long life had been so hospitable no matter what strange creatures were brought into the house – no less so to Tom himself. The leopard had now shown himself in his true colours, and from this point on had to be regarded as a wild cat. Feeling that he might not adapt to more restrictive captivity while surrounded by so many reminders of his young life, John decided to send him away. His last journey was to the open spaces of Longleat, where he remains to this day.

The one animal whose position in the park hierarchy had never been effectively challenged by Tom was Twiggy, the elephant. Her pre-eminence was unassailable and since her arrival as a two-year-old she had ridden high in popularity and esteem. She had a gentle nature and even temper, but a mischievous streak would come to the fore from time to time. Although generally compliant with her keepers' instructions she sometimes insisted on reminding them that she had a will of her own. One of the keepers was one day trying to placate a group of visitors, whom Twiggy had just given a 'dust-bath'.

'It's a funny thing,' he was explaining, 'she sometimes

does that to strangers but never to any of us. I've been her keeper for two years and she's never squirted anything at m—' His last words were smothered in a cloud of dust which hit him full in the face.

Twiggy loved people, and missed them when the season ended. They appealed to her vanity. She was never so happy as when being admired, and, besides, the visitors made such good playmates and foils for her tricks. They looked down into the elephant pit from behind a fence just out of Twiggy's reach, but she would sometimes build up a pile of stones and stand on them so that she could reach over the barrier with her trunk and go through their pockets. It is therefore very difficult to persuade people not to give her things to eat and play with, particularly as Twiggy would help herself if they did not. On one occasion a young visitor passed the pit on a pony, raising her riding hat to Twiggy, who seized it in her trunk, threw it in the air, kicked it into her pool, retrieved it, and trampled it to pulp. Mugged visitors have reported scarves, handbags, wellingtons, umbrellas and once a tartan cap being purloined in this way. Twiggy made an enemy for life of a man who was taking a picture of her to use up a roll of film, the rest of which was devoted to shots of his holiday in Spain: Twiggy whisked the camera away and demolished it. Her pickpocketing activities once yielded a packet of birth pills, a a theft which made her another enemy – or possibly two.

Some visitors claimed that Twiggy looked bored in her pit. In fact, she had two long walks and a swim every day, and always found plenty to do between meals. It is easy to be misled by that mournful expression, but that is what an elephant looks like, even when it's having one helluva time. It is doubtful that she had any strong objections to captivity but if she did she had a very subtle way of expressing them. On several occasions the keepers have been mystified to find the padlock of her stable door was missing at the end of a mucking-out session. The first time this happened her keeper scoured the enclosure and eventually gave up looking. Three days later, as the elephant was about her morning toiletries, he heard a hefty metallic clunk, which seemed to come from Twiggy's nether end. Probing the droppings with his fork he turned up the missing padlock. It is a reflection on the park's constant drive to save money that the padlock is still in use, and that it has twice since embarked on that three-day expedition into the interior and out again. But what the management saved on padlocks, they could spend on elephants, and after four seasons of nothing but human company it was time to get Twiggy a companion of her own kind.

One Easter a lunchtime radio news bulletin ended: '. . . and we have just heard that at this moment a baby elephant on its way to Cricket St Thomas Wild Life Park is crossing London and is breaking up the van in which it is being transported.' This was the first this country heard of the arrival of Chikki – the two-year-old baby elephant. Her transportation was in fact well under control; the bit about 'breaking up the van' had been dreamed up by John, who had fed the information to be sure of getting the park's name on the air. There was, however, an element of truth in it. A two-ton van designed for a calf or two was bound to feel a certain amount of strain when subjected to about its own weight in elephant, particularly when it also had to travel a greater distance than usual – in this case from the Netherlands.

John had bought the elephant from Wassenaar zoo, which did not do deliveries, so he and Jill had to go and collect it. They took the calf van on a night ferry to The Hague, spent the day loading up and arrived back at the Dutch port the following evening. It had been a difficult drive. Not only did the cargo keep shifting its weight in the back of the van, but there was also a gale-force cross-wind to contend with which boded ill for the boat trip. The Dutch port authorities turned out to have their own ideas about subjecting livestock to choppy crossings.

'Vat hev you got in ze beck?' asked a Dutch official with bushy eyebrows.

'An elephant.'

'Oliphant, no?'

'Yes.'

'Heh heh heh,' laughed the Dutchman enjoying the joke. 'Then you must hev a label for your . . . heh heh heh . . . oliphant,' he joked, writing one out and handing it across the desk.

'What do I do with this?'

'You stick it on your . . . heh heh heh oliphant.'

John stepped outside the booth and complied, letting down the ramp and slapping the label on the elephant's backside, and presented himself once more in front of the official.

'Vat hev you done with ze label?'

'I stuck it on the elephant.'

The official nodded soberly, then stiffened up and spoke in an official tone.

'You know ve cannot ship horses.'

'I don't want to ship horses.'

'Too much storm – horses get seasick.'

'I suppose they would.'

'Ve cannot take horses.'

'I haven't got any horses. I've got an elephant.'

'Oliphant,' chuckled the official, savouring the word as it rolled off his upper lip.

Another official with bushier eyebrows, more braid and pips on his uniform bustled up. They jabbered at each other in an animated exchange dominated by the words 'paard' – presumably a horse – and 'oliphant'. They both laughed heartily, then stopped smiling abruptly and approached John with severe faces.

'Ve may not take your horses,' said the pips.

'I haven't got horses. It's an elephant in there.'

The two officials looked at each other, shaking their heads, despairing of making this foreigner see sense. The pips signalled the other to do his duty.

'Open up,' he commanded, marching towards the van. John fiddled with the ramp chains, and the official stood over him confidently, like 'Call my Bluff' panellists about to be declared true or false. The ramp clattered on the tarmac, and the two men gasped.

'It is an oliphant.'

'An oliphant.'

'An oliphant, an oliphant.'

Talking fast and furiously, they ran back into the booth and barked more 'oliphants' down the phone. Within seconds an even more elaborately embroidered uniform appeared, inhabited by a man with even thicker eyebrows, to be briefed by the two officials both talking at once. He brushed them aside and approached John with condescending hauteur.

'Ve do not ship horses,' he said, and glanced into the back of the truck stumbling backwards and blinking.

'It is an oliphant,' he informed his colleagues, who welcomed his authoritative confirmation. Then, peering at the label on Chikki's backside, he reinforced his diagnosis with, 'It says so on the label.'

'It is not a horse,' he confided to John, who did not know whether this was a question or a statement.

'So maybe ve can help. But you must see ze captain. Come wiz me, please.'

A cluster of dock workers was gathering round the back of the van, with the junior official showing off his discovery, as John was marched off to the captain. Within half an hour Chikki was stowed in the hold, and as darkness fell the ferry set sail. There were no horses on board to keep her company, but periodic visits by John found her munching contentedly throughout the journey.

English customs at Harwich were less perturbed by this curiosity.

'Anything to declare?'

'One elephant.'

'No liquor, cigarettes, perfume, jewwellery . . .'

'Just an elephant.'

He thumbed nonchalantly through his regulation book mumbling.

'Elephant, elephant, elepha . . . Oi, Jim – what's the duty on elephants?'

'It's only a small one,' said John humbly.

A voice echoed back across the customs shed, 'I think there's a bit of duty. I'll find out.'

'Wait a minute,' John protested. 'This is for a private collection. There isn't any duty on it.'

The men looked at each other, and decided to let the matter drop. Another official approached the van and asked to see John's tickets. Fumbling through his papers John noticed for the first time that the travel agent in London had made Chikki's ticket out in the name of L. E. Phant. The official noticed it.

'L. E. Phant. Is that the name?'

'That's right,' said John, starting up the van. As he pulled away from the group of officials, he heard the ticket man say:

'Blimey – some parents don't half call their kids some bloody daft names.'

It was early morning and the wind had dropped, but even so the elephant cargo was not making the driving easy. Periodically John peered round through the glass partition window and met the stare of sullen brown eyes from the back. All seemed to be well. John and Jill went on chatting in the front, but Chikki was feeling left out of the conversation. Suddenly there was a splintering crash and a trunk came swishing through the partition into the cab. John instantly recalled his own brochure writings on the subject of elephants' trunks. 'They can tear down a tree, but they can also pick up a nut.' Somewhere between those two extremes lay a capacity to steer a vehicle, change gear, turn the ignition off, start the windscreen wipers or strangle the driver and Chikki at that moment seemed intent on exploring the full range of possibilities. John pulled off the road by a cluster of shops. There were two ways to deal with this situation – either to stop the trunk getting into the cab, or to keep it harmlessly employed. The second seemed to be the easiest solution.

'Have you any bananas?' asked Jill in a small general stores.

'Yes, dear, how many would you like?'

'Twenty. Any apples?'

'Cox's or Golden Delicious?'

'Both – as many as you've got, please.'

'We do a presentation box if you're taking it up to the hospital.'

'No – don't bother. I'll have some pears too. Five pounds.'

'Have a good party, dear,' said the grocer.

For the next hour or so Chikki's trunk was manageable. Jill sat with a box of fruit on her knees and the trunk shuffled back and forth through the partition with bananas, apples and pears without once straying into the driver's side of the cab. One or two trunk signals out of the nearside windows, meaning anything from 'Please overtake on the inside' to 'I am about to turn three somersaults and turn left', confused the occasional motorist, but the ploy was working well. They were in London before the supply of fruit had run out, and the trunk had started to harass the driver again, nuzzling his ear, pulling his sunglasses off and tugging his hair. As it was Sunday, buying more fruit was not so easy, as there did not seem to be a shop open anywhere nearby. The only place in the area which offered any promise of salvation was the B B C T V Centre. John drove through the gates and pulled up outside one of the scenery department workshops. The curious workings of the B B C seem to make provision for eventualities of this sort. The television centre remains about the only place where John has taken any of his animals where they have aroused no surprise or interest whatever. The sudden appearance of an elephant in the middle of the workshop seemed to be, for all the excitement it caused, a perfectly normal event. Fixing a plywood replacement for the broken partition window was done with alacrity and efficiency by a man whose permanent job appeared to be 'elephant truck window replacer for the B B C (Television)'. The job done, John drove off, half expecting another elephant truck to drive into the bay behind him marked 'For the Attention of E T W R, B B C (T V)'. Compared with the last hundred miles, the next hundred and thirty miles were bliss. Chikki arrived to a tumultuous welcome from a reception committee of staff, visitors and press, and was led off to her new home.

Such an enthusiastic welcome for the new baby elephant could be guaranteed, but the success of the last stage of her homecoming could not. This depended on Twiggy. After all, Twiggy was seven years old and had not seen another elephant for several years, and there was no knowing how she might react to the newcomer. Even if she took to her new companion, Chikki might not take to her. So the introduction would be an anxious moment, and all the keepers were assembled to supervise it. Twiggy had already been chained up when Chikki was led into the stable. She did not react at all. If she felt any surprise, affinity, or even curiosity, she was giving nothing away. For a time she pretended she had not seen the new arrival, and turned away. Chikki was equally non-committal, and allowed herself to be tethered out of reach of the other elephant. There had been none of the feared animosity, which with animals so huge might have been difficult to handle, and at least now the two elephants were safe from each other. But it was still not prudent to leave them alone. Three keepers stayed with them all night, taking it in turns to watch, while the other two cat-napped on bales of straw. Twiggy remained aloof and stand-offish, but after a few hours Chikki began to be inquisitive. She started edging over towards the older elephant and trying to attract her attention. Twiggy was still immovable, but Chikki was persistent, and began to tug at her tether until her efforts to rid herself of her shackles became frantic. It was not all that long ago that Chikki had been separated from her herd, and the keepers, interpreting her struggling as a desire for the warmth of a mother, decided to take the plunge. They loosened her chains slowly, led her forward and stood back as the young elephant snuggled up to her new mother figure. Twiggy made no objection.

It was an anti-climax. Had there been any antagonism the eruption would have been monumental, and it seemed reasonable to expect a successful meeting to be hugely demonstrative, but that was not Twiggy's way. She took to her new companion gradually, the transition from cool detachment to abiding affection taking months. She became protective, calmer, more adult and undoubtedly the boss. Chikki was playful and mischievous, swinging on the beams of the stable, dismantling the waterpipes, turning the taps on and off and chewing the plaster. Yet it was Twiggy who took the lead in the rough and tumble when they were on their outings. These consisted of a 'dawn patrol' – a walk round the estate in the early mornings – and a swim in one of the lakes in the mid-afternoons. For the morning run they are taken up to the woodlands where they play hide-and-seek between the trees, swing on the branches, and skate down the banks. They know roughly what is allowed and when, and are generally obedient to the keepers, but their loyalties are divided since they have had a number of different keepers in their time, and the only constant factor in their lives has been John. If the keeper is leading them home, and John happens to be walking in the other direction, they will sometimes turn round and follow him. And it works the other way round. On one occasion John was supervising their excursion to the woods and Peter started up a tractor for the food-run outside their stable, some half a mile away. They stopped dead in their tracks, fanned out their big ears, turned towards the sound, and trumpeted a reply in a deafening nasal chorus:

'We're here.'

And they set off home.

7

One Thing on Top of Another

'Come quickly – the donkey and the goat are stuck together,'
announced Celia one morning, bursting into the office. It
was an unfortunate choice of words. Reports which come
into the house of animals being stuck together usually allude
to dogs, and it is a polite way of saying that they are mating.
But here was the intimation that a donkey and a goat were
conjoining in the delights of love, so the news elicited more
than usual curiosity. But the event did not make the zoological history it at first seemed to promise. Far from the
two animals showing themselves to be more than usually
compatible, it became clear that they had fallen out. The
donkey had kicked out at the goat, and got its back leg
inextricably caught in its horns. Both were immobilized.
The donkey was hobbling around on three legs using the
goat as a sort of roller-skate for the fourth.

'It's one thing on top of another,' said Paddy, separating
hoof and horns like a Chinese puzzle. He did not mean it
as a literal description of the present situation, but as an
expression of irritation at being suddenly dragged off in
the middle of what he had been doing to attend to this
minor emergency. It happened all too often. Running a
wild-life park is not one of those jobs in which one can
settle down to a day's work without fear of being interrupted
and side-tracked. What is more, most of the reports which
come into the office call for immediate attention. 'Drop
everything and investigate' is the rule rather than the exception. That is why anybody working in the office lives in
awe of the phone and the doorbell.

The phone is less alarming than the doorbell. Although there is always a chance that a caller may be reporting an escape, the telephone is largely the medium of routine matters which are dealt by Gwen, the secretary. However, some callers ring the park for the oddest reasons.

'West Country Wild Life Park,' says Gwen.

'Hello, can I speak to Mr C. Lion, please?'

'Oh no, not another,' Gwen thinks.

'I've got a message to call a Mr C. Lion at that number.'

'I'm afraid you've been had,' says Gwen politely.

She has had several callers asking to speak to non-existent people with animal names. Somewhere nearby lived a joker fast losing his friends by giving them these names and the number, which they were not to know was the Wild Life Park. Mr C. Lion was his favourite, but Mr G. Raffe, Mr L. E. Fant and Mr E. Mew were apparently also on the Cricket payroll. Gwen also had to deal with many other weird phone calls. Of all the extraordinary requests made of the park, the one made by the organisers of a Christmas party at a nearby naval base was perhaps the most bizarre.

'Can we borrow a reindeer?' enquired one of those cut-glass naval voices at the other end of the line.

'What do you want a reindeer for?'

'We're having a children's party and we want a reindeer to bring Father Christmas in.'

'I'm afraid we haven't got a reindeer.'

'Well, have you got a moose or a deer or something?'

'Not one that would take kindly to being strapped up to a sleigh. I don't think we've got anything that tame.'

'Pity. Haven't you got anything at all we could use?'

'We've got a stuffed moose head.'

Eventually, Tom, the leopard cub, deputized for the reindeer. As all the phone calls come from outside the estate, in other words outside the park's jurisdiction, one can answer it with a measure of confidence that it will not mean trouble. Not so the doorbell. When there is a spot of bother on the estate it will come right to the door.

'Drrrrring!'

'That sounds like one of the keepers,' says John, his identification confounded by the entry of an irate gardener.

'It's those perishing peacocks again,' says the gardener. 'Straight through the tulips.'

The wild-life park, the farms and the gardens often find themselves at loggerheads, and when they work at cross-purposes and conflict quarrels have to be patched up. The gardeners and the peacocks have never been the best of friends. A peacock standing innocently by a flower-bed only has to turn round to lay low an arc of tulips with its tail, though walking straight through a flower-bed is more characteristic. Similarly, the wading birds in the tropical aviary wreak havoc with the exotic vegetation with their clumsy webbed tramping. Nor are the elephants any garden lovers. They are not particularly scrupulous about covering their tracks, but somebody has to, and no gardener relishes the job. Despite every effort to keep them on the paths, if they walk two abreast there is bound to be a casualty or two among the verges and beds. If they choose to take a slide down a daffodilled bank, prune a tree, or shred a hedge, there is not much you can do about it except apologize to the gardeners afterwards.

'Dring-dring!'

'That'll be the gamekeeper for me,' says Paddy.

In fact it is one of the herdsmen complaining about the elephants going on the cows' pastures. They had also started a stampede of the cattle.

'I'll see they don't chase the cows again,' John promises.

'They weren't chasing the cows. The cows were chasing them,' says the herdsman.

These elephants have curiously selective sight. They see cows, but they do not appear to see horses. Another herdsman has had occasion to complain about a sarus crane starting a stampede. A crane in full flight is an awesome sight – four foot of bird suspended between six feet of wing – and one had swooped down across the pastures blotting out the sun and set the whole herd of cows a-gallop. Cows seem to have selective fear; they are scared of big birds, but not of elephants.

'Ding!' This one sounded like the head-keeper's distinctive ring.

'This'll be for me,' says Paddy. But in walks the gamekeeper, and for John. The elephants are in trouble again. On their walks they had been trampling over the pheasants' 'feed-ride' – a strip of straw running through the woods which is sprinkled with corn to entice the birds out of their release pen. The elephants had been bodging it full of holes.

'Have the pheasants been falling into them, then?'

'No,' says the gamekeeper. 'But I have.'

The office is not the focal point of the Wild Life Park alone, but also of its allied operations – a catering establishment, a retail business and the four farms. Through it parades an endless calvacade of representatives, salesmen, inspectors, accountants, keepers, farm workers, job applicants and visitors with scores to settle with the management. It is in the 'Big House' and, being in the old butler's pantry, it is strategically placed to serve the rest of the building. Moreover, it provides a useful short cut between one half of the house and the other, a fact which children, dogs and various other family strays have cottoned on to. From time to time the office becomes a bedlam of cross-talk and crossed-wires, and household and estate activities have to be disentangled.

'What is this place, a crèche, kennels or Hyde Park Corner?' exclaims Paddy when the room is dense with wives, children and dogs – a broad hint that the grand dispersal should begin.

'D-dring!'

'Bet that isn't one of the keepers,' says John as one of the keepers throws open the door.

'The swoose's father is dead,' he declares.

This was sad news, although it was a relief that the deceased was not the swoose itself.

A swoose, as would seem obvious, is a cross between a swan and a goose, a unique combination, albeit a more plausible coupling than a goat and a donkey. It looks like a goose with superb feathers or a swan with a very short neck, whichever way you prefer to look at it. In fact, the combination is not as strange as it sounds, and many people have walked past this creature without observing that there is something odd about it. But on the other hand there are many who have, and this is why it came to Cricket. This swoose is the only one of its kind. It formerly lived on a Ministry of Defence pond near a plastics factory on an industrial estate a few miles away. What the Ministry was up to on that pond nobody knows, but they were anxious not to draw attention to themselves. Nor did they have to so long as Willie the swoose was there to do the attention-seeking for them, and factory girls used to stroll on to the Ministry of Defence property to see this rare specimen. So the Ministry regarded the creature as a security risk and gave it to Cricket. But Willie was not alone. He brought his father Charlie the gander with him, but the pen (the female swan), which was Willie's mother, was sent to another lake the other end of Somerset. Willie took well enough to his new surroundings, but not so his father. Within a week he was dead. The keeper had found him lying on the surface of the lake. There were no marks on him and the post-mortem revealed nothing. The actual cause of death remains unknown, but it was not considered a mystery since there was a perfectly good reason for him to die, even though it would not rate as a scientifically established verdict. That was that Charlie died of a broken heart as a result of being separated from his mate. The fact that the two of them had produced a unique bird (a swoose) must have given them more cause for mutual affection and strengthened their relationship beyond the normal requirements of birds pairing. This is roughly how the story appeared in the newspapers at the time, and no doubt many local tears were shed on Charlie's behalf. One thing the papers left out was what the post-mortem did reveal. That was that Charlie was not Swoose's father. He was his mother. Another first?

Charlie's funeral march was a solitary 'D-dring' on the

108

park office doorbell, an instrument which takes on a more triumphant note when keepers arrive to proclaim the birth of a llama, or a camel, or a lynx. But the event which really sets both the phone and the doorbell off, clamorous and persistent, is an escape. There has never been a really dramatic escape from Cricket – one which threatens the neighbourhood, like the disappearance of a puma or a leopard, and which calls for a massive police search or captures the indignant attentions of local authorities and the newspapers. Yet escapes are going on all the time. The fugitives are mainly birds. Most of those which are allowed to go free, like the parakeets, have the good sense not to go too far since the park offers the best food in the district. But a few quaker parakeets, a couple of white storks and cranes and conures have escaped and bred quite satisfactorily in the wild, and local people ring in news of their progress. Some have not been so lucky, for instance the odd flamingo which had not been pinioned properly has flown away and perished.

Notable among the 'go it alone' merchants was a wallaby, which vanished without trace, and pregnant at that. Prairie dogs burrow out from time to time, and may or may not survive. But neither prepared to stay nor to go away completely are the beavers. A pair of beavers were among the earliest arrivals at the park coming from Edinburgh Zoo, and they were given their own woodland enclosure by the lakes. Beavers, being industrious, hyperactive creatures, at once turn their living quarters into a building site which, as every navvy knows, is a source of public fascination. These beavers, however, did not know this, and, unaware of their public responsibilities, did all their best work in secret, proving somewhat uncooperative and self-effacing exhibits. Furthermore, they lost no time in digging their way to freedom through the banks of the lake. Destructive creatures that they are, one seldom sees a beaver, though one can always see where they have been. Forde Abbey, a historic estate two miles west of Cricket, soon bore the telltale scare of beaverdom, and, being a nursery estate, sabotage by beavers was something which they could well do without. A number of posses were sent out after them, each one drawing a blank. A temporary truce was followed by a resurgence of terrorism, this time in woodland on the east side of the park, where the beavers had dammed the drainage arrangements by a duckpond, flooding an adjoining farm road. After complaints from the Council and water-treading pedestrians the chase was revived, but once again the fugitives went to ground. Their next appearance was impertinent in its cunning, for they turned up at the very lakeside from which they had originally escaped, no doubt to give the impression they had been there all the time. Determined not to be outwitted again, John launched an elaborate anti-beaver operation and pounced on them at dead of night with Henry and his tractor and winch and all the necessary hardware to drain the lake, in which they were in hiding. This done, the recidivists were still nowhere to be found, and remain at large to this day. As escapers, these beavers are in a class by themselves, because the only reason for wanting them captured is to get rid of them, which is an unrewarding and negative motive. Their performance as park attractions has been spectacularly disappointing and while no one wishes them any harm, the intention is only to send them to another park or zoo where they might be more appreciated. If, beavers, you ever read this . . .

One of the more bizarre escape adventures on record, the foiled attempt for freedom of Gert the sealion, was still to come, but her companion Bert made a dummy run or two. Along the trough of the valley nine lakes are formed by a trickling tributary of the River Axe, all on different levels and separated by weirs. The sealions were supposed to be on the top lake, but it seemed that however spacious the accommodation you give a sealion it will always want to be somewhere else. Bert clambered over the first weir and was carried by the gentle current to the next, and over that to the bottom lake. But by then he had run out of lakes by which to continue his descent and the next weir took him into a shallow stream running under the sawmills, where his path was blocked by an immovable waterwheel which used to power the mills. Getting back up to the lakes again was something he had not considered until that moment, and, accepting that it was beyond his ingenuity, there he stayed. It was the woodman who found him the next morning, having spent a very uncomfortable night in the mud under the sawmills. The sealion salvaging operation was complicated. Nobody could get to him in his inaccessible gully and no amount of extra fish rations could coax him out. The recapturing party had to wait for him to emerge in his own good time, and enticing him back up the valley by land was an expedition which took several weeks.

Few escape adventures can match that of one of the monkeys. The monkeys are all characters in their way, but none so extrovert as an eccentric old capuchin. Keepers are always on their guard when opening the cage doors in the morning to deliver breakfasts, but there is little they can do if a monkey decides to make a dash for it. This particular capuchin, never one to premeditate his actions, one morning saw his chance and leapt for the half-open door. Too fast, and too strong in mid-leap to brook much opposition, he was suddenly free. Crouching on the ground, he let the keeper approach him, but as soon as he was within touching distance, the monkey leapt up on to the parapet round the raccoon pit and jumped up and down, chattering the monkey equivalent of 'Can't catch me!' His next leap, on the keeper's advance, was on to the top of his own cage. This backed on to a barn the other side of the walled garden, and had he got on top of the barn and down the other side he would have sealed himself off from his pursuers and run loose in the farm. Knowing this, the keeper was not anxious to continue the chase and thought it best to bide his time and coax him down from the top of the cage. The monkey, however, did not think that this was much fun and wanted to keep the game going, so he leapt from there and began to swing on the electric cable running along the eaves of the barn. He then bit the cable. There was a blinding blue flash and the monkey plummeted ten feet to the ground and lay motionless. He was rushed to the kitchens and the vet was called. Every attempt was made to revive him, but the creature did not respond. No heartbeat, no pulse, no breathing. The monkey was laid to rest in a box of straw. His obsequies were all but over when the vet arrived.

'Too late,' said the keeper, 'he's dead. We did everything we could.'

'Am I in time for the post-mortem?' said the vet.

'He's in there,' said the keeper, indicating the box of straw as the vet prepared his instruments. A faint rustle issued from the box, then a hand appeared over the side followed by a pair of frightened eyes, all belonging to a very animate monkey which took one look at the vet with his razors and shot out of the box and through the door like an electric shock. Within seconds it was back at its cage, rattling the weld-mesh pleading to be let in. The keeper opened the door for it and the monkey hopped inside as eagerly as it had burst out. This monkey must be the only escaped animal which ever died to tell the tale.

8

Homo Sapiens –
This Animal Bites

If the family's lack of experience with wild animals had been an initial disadvantage, their previous lack of dealings with 'The Public' had in many ways proved a greater handicap.

Of the quarter of a million people who visit every season, most come and go without doing more than enjoy everything Cricket has to offer. The visitors one remembers are the exceptions – the people who with a remark or an observation, a complaint or an expression of praise, an indiscretion or a display of carelessness, contribute to the fund of memorable occurrences which make the day-to-day life at the park so varied and entertaining or at times scary.

'I think it's disgusting,' explodes an irate mother, storming out of the milking parlour viewing gallery, tugging a child with his bobble hat pulled down over his eyes.

'What's that?' asks one of the gardeners, unbending from a rosebed by the neighbouring monkey cage.

'I think it's immoral that you should allow children to watch that man feeling those cows' bosoms.'

There was no answer to this outburst.

'You can tell the manager I said so,' the woman went on.

'I *am* the manager,' said Paddy, quite used to being taken for the gardener. 'I'm sorry,' he said meekly. It was a sincere apology. If the illusion – surprisingly prevalent – that milk grows on doorsteps had not been dispelled, the park was at fault. Education was part of its purpose. He made a note to install a 'talking label' in the gallery to explain the processes of milking. This conversation took place only a matter of days since another woman had registered a protest about the flamingoes which she had seen in a flock in the shallows of the lake standing, to a man, on one leg.

'It's very cruel,' she had expostulated, drubbing her finger on John's desk. 'What right have you to do such a thing to one of God's creatures!'

'What?'

'Cutting off one of their legs to stop them running away.'

Most complaints are a bit more reasonable. It is one thing seeing the animals and feeling confident that they are well fed and content, but it is another thing seeing the remains of young chicks in a vulture's cage or rats in the snake's case which have been slaughtered for feeding. To anyone these sights seem irksome, but these are the facts of life – a humane simulation of the ways of the wild – but not everybody sees it that way. Nor is there any attempt to hide them. John spends much of his time patiently explaining the hard truths of animal keeping. Once it was to an outraged woman who had made a special journey from some miles away to speak her mind.

'I saw this leopard and it was eating a goat,' she grumbled.

'He likes goats,' said John.

'Do your leopards always eat goats?'

'Not unless one dies. That one died of old age. It seemed a pity to waste it.'

'Oh,' said the woman, the wind take out of her sails.

'I don't suppose the goat would have minded very much,' said John as a prelude to a fuller explanation of the workings of a wild-life park. The plaintiff accepted it with surprising good humour, and they parted the best of friends.

'If I get any more dead goats I'll send them to you.'

'No – please don't do that,' she laughed, as she left the office.

This lady was one of many visitors who had taken the trouble to write in after their visit to express their unease about animal captivity. This sort of correspondence is welcomed and John deals with every letter himself to dispel their disquiet as fully as necessary, often adding an invitation to come and discuss their observations in more detail. A few take him up on it. The brochure makes it clear that suggestions are always appreciated, and letters come, not only complaining that the elephants look bored, that the leopards look miserable, or that the monkeys have not enough greenery, but suggesting remedies.

Many of them accuse the park of not looking at the situation from the caged animal's point of view, when this is precisely what the complainers themselves are guilty of. Forgetting that they are not animals, they see themselves spending their lives in the cage, in which case it would be disagreeable; but for an animal captivity can be a very comfortable easy existence. Some of the correspondents even go so far as to suggest remedies. One schoolboy, a budding architect, even went so far as to design a complete penguin pit and landscaped 'natural boundaries' for all the enclosures to replace the chain-link fencing.

Many of the improvements recommended, like the enlargement of an enclosure, are already 'in hand', or on the list of things to be done. However, but for the letters, some minor hazards, like an insecure length of fencing or a loose branch of a tree in the picnic area, might never be noticed. For these important reports one is dependent on public observation. Some are acted upon at once. Between the garden and the elephant pit there is a long low dark tunnel in which tropical fish tanks have been embedded in the walls. One man wrote in to say that he was so intrigued by the fish that that he did not see a protuding stone from the roof, and being six foot two cracked his head on it; within a day the tunnel was a clearway for seven footers. Other suggestions you cannot do much about.

Dear Mr Office Man,
    Please would you tell me why did you put the aquarium in the tunnel because many people are scared to go in and see the fish. My mum was.
                                    Love from Leslie.

It was sad to have to take issue with Leslie, writing so thoughtfully on behalf of 'many people'. His mum was an exception, and until her timidity reaches epidemic proportions, shifting the fish must make way for priorities.

Some considered recommendations come from authoritative sources, pointing out minor weaknesses in the operation, but none devastatingly condemning. Others come from impassioned animal lovers from houses named 'The Savanna' or 'The Waterhole', whose misinformed fulminations give an account as to why they have never actually visited the place. Questions like 'Why do you spoil all your beautiful fields with cow manure?' can be politely dismissed; observations like 'The pony giving children rides does not get enough time off' can be investigated; objections that 'Some of your birds are labelled wrongly' can be checked. 'That is not a heron,' writes Mrs E. R. of 'The Pampas', Tiverton. 'Herons do not have a dark blue streak of feathers.' And then there's a letter or two about the controversial hollow sausage rolls.

But nestling in the mass of correspondence are letters which raise a spectre which constantly haunts wild-life park operators. That is public safety. To what extent is the security of visitors compatible with the freedom of animals? It would be very easy to impound every animal with double fencing or two sets of bars instead of one, but that would ruin the view of the animals and spoil the look of their natural habitats. On the other hand one could let all the animals roam free and cage the people up, but that would have the same effect. It would cease to be a wild-life park. Allowing people to mingle as freely as possible with the animals is a calculated risk which both management and visitors must be prepared to take. As a rule, this is mutually understood, but every so often an animal or a visitor steps out of line. If an emu nips a child's hand or a camel eats somebody's hat, or a mynah bird pecks at a protruding finger, most victims accept that they may have asked for it, but they write in after the event when they feel somebody ought to be told.

The newspaper headline 'Child mauled by Puma at Cricket St Thomas' and subsequent radio and television reports made the park's security arrangements look inadequate. Far from deterring visitors the reports, oddly enough, increased the gate. Plainly the incident called for a thorough investigation which showed that it was not so sinister as it was made out. Surrounding the puma cage there was a five-foot flower-bed between the pathway and the bars. A three-year-old child had detached herself from her parents, scrambled over the bed and started climbing up the bars. A puma sprang at her, and the child was so frightened that she bit her tongue, the only injury which called for hospital treatment. One cannot blame the child or the puma, but accept that there were shortcomings in both the safety precautions and in the parents' surveillance.

This incident is about the most serious lapse of security which has happened at Cricket, and the installation of a low outer barricade outside the surrounding flower-bed was still no fail-safe guarantee that it will not happen again unless a measure of sound sense and caution from the visitors can also be ensured. You can put warning notices up all over the bars until the animals are obliterated altogether, but there will still be people who choose to ignore them. Their tone can be strengthened a bit. John once had to substitute the inscription 'This animal may bite' for 'This animal bites' in the light of his own harsh experience.

John's answer to reports of fateful encounters between people and animals where it is obvious that the visitor is at fault is to remind them that this is a *wild*-life park and that no creature can be altogether trusted or treated as if it were a pussy cat or a budgie. Even he and the keepers, who have over the years built up close and trusting relationships with their charges, have to remind themselves of this from time to time. If they do not, the animals themselves jog their memories. Blood drawn by an angry monkey, an overzealous bite from the leopard cub, or an uncharacteristic tantrum from one of the elephants, sometimes tells them exactly where they stand.

All animals are largely unpredictable, and there are times when their departures from their normal patterns of behaviour occur at the worst possible moments. Although animals and keepers become firm friends, great companions for fun and games, the relations can never be on equal terms – particularly if your playmate is an elephant. One of the greatest attractions of the summer afternoons is the sight of Peter or John taking Twiggy and Chikki down to the lake for their daily swim. They play follow-my-leader on the quarter-mile tramp from their enclosure, occasionally stopping to rub themselves against a tree or to pick a flower, the procession gathering a crowd led by a sort of safari pied-piper. The patrol then goes into the sealion enclosure, where the elephants slide down a muddy groove cut into the bank and into the water where they wallow and splash each other. It was after this swim one day when the elephants had emerged and were making their way through the spectators who stood back as they trundled forward, that a man ran in front of them to take a photograph. Twiggy suddenly broke into a trot and was after him. She was heading straight for the man as he ran backwards in her path taking his picture, and although she slowed down she showed no signs of stopping.

'Don't move – she'll stop if you stay put,' yelled the keeper running up behind. 'Whoa! Whoa!' Twiggy usually heeded this instruction, but not this time. A mighty swish of her trunk and the photographer was sprawling on the ground. As he scrambled to his feet Twiggy was drawing back for another assault. The man slipped in the mud and was down again making him a sitting duck as Twiggy moved forward.

'Back! Back!' shrieked the keeper, not yet quite ahead of her. The crowd stood rigid and looked on aghast.

It was Chikki who saved the day. She honed in and intercepted the charge, delivering a hefty broadside with her forehead, which had Twiggy reeling off course. The incident ended as abruptly as it had begun. The two elephants nuzzled each other without apparent ill-feeling, while the keeper berated Twiggy with stern blows across the bridge of her trunk. Something had obviously upset her, and there was no doubt that she had something personal against the man she had placed within inches of his life. He did not seem to realize the danger he was in, and curiously enough appeared to revel in the episode, his main concern being for his camera which had fallen in the mud. The crowd, seconds before filled with delight and amusement, was now thundering with righteous indignation. The brunt of it fell on the keeper, who was the obvious target for accusations against the park which had allowed the public to be inveigled into the presence of his 'rogue' elephant. After the ugliest scene in his whole lifetime with animals the keeper breathed a sigh of relief when he turned the key in the padlock of the elephants' enclosure after a nasty and flustered retreat. Allowing the visitors to mingle so freely with even such habitually gentle creatures had shown itself to be a risk not worth taking, and thereafter visitors have to content themselves with watching the elephant dip from a discreet distance.

Nevertheless, the elephants are still brought out under strict supervision for special occasions, as are some other animals normally confined to their quarters. What's more they seem to know when 'a special occasion' is in the offing, and behave marginally differently in its honour.

One morning at the height of the season, a theatre publicity agent rang up wanting a location for a series of *TV Times* feature pictures of a number of television stars currently appearing at the end of Somerset piers. John threw a lunch party for them the following Sunday. If ever a meal was like 'feeding time at the zoo', this was it. This is no reflection on the table manners of the guests, but it is doubtful whether such a noisy bunch of extroverts was ever assembled round one table.

The company, particularly one Irish comic, perpetrated one awful gag after another, which was picked up and often topped by others. Tom was leaping about under their feet.

'Does he bite?' asked one of the singers.

'No – but he'll give you a nasty suck,' said the Irishman.

'Here, boy. My Mrs has got one like you hanging up in her wardrobe.'

'Teeth and all,' bellowed someone across the room.

'We've got one just like you on the back seat of our car.'

'So *that's* why I get my eyes scratched out every time I try something in the back seat of your car.'

There is often cause for house guests to complain about the noise coming from the animals, but there is seldom cause for the animals to complain about the noise coming from the house. This was the exception. The animals were naturally curious and growls of speculation were transmitted from cage to cage.

Soon John led the party into the walled garden followed by a bevy of photographers.

'What's that over there?'

'It's a rare duck.'

'Good – I like my duck rare.' The banter went on.

The reaction of some of the animals to a camera is usually interesting. While they don't exactly rush indoors to smarten themselves up they do realize that their existence is about to be immortalized and seem anxious to create a good impression. Some of the monkeys will climb to the highest branch of their trees and assume some precarious contortion, which they can just hold long enough for the shutters to click, and then plummet helplessly to the ground. Others bring out their young and pose as a family group. Twiggy had already demolished a camera or two when she did not feel up to it. Fariq, the camel, could usually summon up the good manners to stop slobbering. The sealions think that some kind of noise is called for and lift their heads in the air to bark. Peacocks are seldom cooperative. That is not to say they do not like being photographed but they regard the comment which always goes with an amateur picture of a peacock, 'We couldn't get it to fan out its tail', as some kind of compliment to their integrity and disdain for the media.

It was with remarkable esprit de corps that on this particular star-studded afternoon the animals attempted to sabotage any photography, when they discovered that the cameras were not exclusively for them. This became obvious to them as the line of famous faces filed past the cages, and the day's visitors suddenly lost interest in the animals, turned, poked each other, and pointed, identifying the new arrivals. The comparison between being a caged zoo animal, and being a T V star was at once apparent. But the animals detailed to pose with these show-biz luminaries were not going to be upstaged, and they entered into a conspiracy of non-cooperation. Twiggy stubbornly refused to allow one of the actresses to sit on her back, and kept wriggling until she fell off. Another of the stars was an impressario who had made a name for himself with a chicken impersonation. He adapted this celebrated routine for a macaw, much to Foot-tapper's indignation, and was bitten on the ear for his trouble. Meanwhile, Tom Leopard was giving one of the actors some of his nastiest sucks, and one of a pair of baby fawns posing with a trio of singers, while putting up a good front, was fouling the group from behind.

'What a critic,' said one of the comics.

The events of that afternoon showed that the animals were capable of registering their objections when subjected to the indignities of a human world. They had exhibited wisdom and judgement, which is more than can be said for some of the visitors who take liberties with the animals. Every wild-life park has its evidence of public irresponsibility and fool-hardiness – like giving monkeys apples full of razor blades. This notorious outrage did not occur at Cricket, although on one occasion somebody gave a monkey an open flick knife to play with. No harm came to that monkey, but a gibbon which accepted the donation of a lollipop was not so lucky. It died of food poisoning.

In another fateful accident which showed that one cannot always rely on the good sense of all visitors, the culprits were a group of unsupervised and meddlesome teenage schoolboys. Raccoons are nocturnal and spend much of the day sleeping in a little tree house made out of an old barrel, waking up at feeding time. Their next-door neighbours, the pumas, take their evening meal in the cages at the back of their enclosure, after which they like to go to sleep. The raccoons, however, are ready for action, and with the pumas safely shut away, they are transferred from their own small pit to spend the night foraging in the puma pen. Meanwhile, the pumas can still be visited by the back entrance, and it is round this other side that the pulleys for opening and shutting the connecting door between cage and enclosure are situated. It was just before closing time one summer evening that one of the schoolboys climbed over the barrier intended to keep people at a safe distance from the puma-cage bars, pulled the cable and released two pumas. He could not see from there what he had done, but within seconds two raccoons had been torn apart. It is inevitable that the park has to take the consequences and blame for an incident like this, although it was blatant vandalism which showed up this minor flaw in an arrangement which worked well for several years.

The business of apportioning blame for an accident might have been clarified if another incident had ever come to court. We will never even know if it would have happened at all, but it may only have been the timely intervention of one of the farm workers which prevented what could have been an ugly scene. Always keeping a watchful eye on visitors, he caught sight of a man about to drop a little terrier dog into the porcupine pen.

'What do you think you're doing?' he asked.

'Oh, nothing,' said the man. 'I just wanted to see what would happen.'

The little dog was squealing blue murder with the three porcupines queueing up underneath ready to receive it. There's no knowing what would have happened if the man had been allowed to continue with his experiment but even the king of the jungle does not take on a porcupine. Those spikes would be in him before he knew what had hit him, and would probably incapacitate him for the rest of his life. Porcupine injuries are among the main causes for lions' attacks on humans in the wild; a lame beast could not catch anything but slow-moving prey. The terrier seemed to sense something of this sort, but not its owner.

For all the individualists who visit the park, the main body of the visitors are eminently well behaved and co-operative. 'The Public' has a personality of its own. It has to be treated delicately. Over the years, the management have discovered that the visitors like to be guided and molly-coddled but do not like being ordered about. There is a barn on one of the farms which is now choc-a-bloc full of old notices saying do this, do that, go here, don't do this, don't go there, which used to litter the estate. They were taken down because people did not take much notice of them, and wanted to feel free. And so they should be. Only the signposts and the essential 'This animal is dangerous', and 'Do not feed', signs survived that purge of notices. However many of them there may be, there will still be people who interpret them as an instruction to risk a finger or offer a currant bun. One or two others had to be re-phrased to have impact. Cricket's 'No Litter' signs were replaced by 'Children – please ensure that your parents do not drop litter', a ploy which worked. Another Cricket sign made its mark on the world by appearing in *The Times*, in its long-running series of odd notices. On the exit road from the park visitors are confronted with the instruction 'Please slow down to allow cows to pass'. It sounds as if cars are likely to be overtaken by stampeding road-hogging herds; what it actually means is that if motorists meet a herd on its way to milking, they can keep going slowly and the cows will walk round them. The way to stop visitors running wild is to keep them interested, so the bulk of the notices aim to give them as much information about the animals and identification assistance as possible. Each pen and enclosure has to be well labelled with the names of its occupants, outline drawings and a bit of information. Thus, as well as enjoying a day at the park visitors can really benefit from it and go home the wiser. This is the purpose for which a great majority of them come. While some visitors show spectacular ignorance and amuse keepers with their comments and wild mis-identifications of animals, each day's inflow also produces a quota of remarkably well-informed and questioning people.

'Look, they've got the walruses we asked for,' said a twelve-year-old in a family group at the lakeside.

'No, they're sealions,' corrected his mother.

'What's the difference?'

'Ask your father – he'll know.'

The boy turned to a man in a tartan hat, awaiting clarification.

'A walrus has much less hair, and it has tusks it uses digging for shell-fish.'

A younger girl chipped in. 'They look like seals to me.'

'No,' the father explained. 'Sealions have ears, seals don't.'

'Yaaagghhhh,' barked one of the sealions.

'Who'd want ears if that's what they have to hear all day,' said the mother.

'Look at those three. They've got ears – that's how you can tell they're sealions.'

'Don't look much like lions to me,' grumbled the small boy.

'You wouldn't expect them to,' objected a teenage brother, 'any more than you'd expect elephant seals to look like elephants.'

'Elephant seals?' queried the girl. 'They'd have tusks, I suppose.'

'No, stupid. If they had tusks they'd be walruses,' snapped the younger boy.

'Not if they had ears.'

The argument continued as the family moved along the valley, through the tunnel and out to the elephant pit. Twiggy was giving herself a hay-sauna, and Chikki was rubbing her tusks against a wooden post.

'Look – the little one's digging for shell-fish,' the young girl exclaimed.

'Eh?' The family rounded on her.

'I thought you said that's what tusks are for?'

'That's only if you're a walrus.'

'Not much like elephant seals, are they,' the twelve-year-old complained. 'I thought you said elephant seals had lots of hair; there's no hair on an elephant, and no tusks on a seal. It beats me.' The older brother, obviously a budding zoologist, could explain everything.

'It's the nose. Elephants have trunks and elephant seals have big noses. Look, you can tell a lot from looking at the Latin name. What's the Latin name, Dad?'

'Order *Proboscidae*,' said the man in the tartan cap.

'You seem to know more than we do,' said John, who had overheard the conversation. 'Are you in the animal game?'

'No – I just got interested. I've picked up a bit over the years.'

'Have you been before?'

'Every year since you opened,' said the wife, proudly. 'We must have been about the first people in.'

'You've seen some changes then,' said John.

'I should say so,' agreed the man. 'Tell you the truth, we didn't like it much at first.'

'Nor did we,' John admitted.

'We often write in and tell you what we think,' said the wife.

'Your elephant pinched his cap one year.'

'So that was yours – we've still got it somewhere.'

'Keep it – I've got a new one.'

'Any complaints this time?'

'Can't think of one off-hand,' said the man.

'No – it's a heavenly place,' his wife declared.

'See you next year then,' said John.

As the family wandered on John overheard the wife say: 'I think we ought to write them a letter.'

'Why?' enquired the man in the tartan cap. 'You haven't got a complaint, have you? Your sausage roll wasn't hollow, was it?'

'No, but I think I'll drop them a line, just the same.'

9

Paradise Lost

Heavenly – that's what the lady said. It was early the following morning, a Monday and for the park staff 'a parson's weekend'. The valley looked deserted compared with the previous two days, and even the animals seemed to know that they had a few days' respite in which to compose themselves for the next weekend rush of visitors. John was on his early round, and savoured the feeling of calm and serenity which suffused the parklands. The animals and birds had begun their day's mingling, breaking away from their night-time kind-by-kind groupings. A barnacle goose was stalking a deer, and a rhea and a llama seemed to be in conversation over a fence. The two elephants were being led by a keeper on their dawn patrol along the top of a far ridge, silhouetted against the rising sun. The camels were having a lie-in, and a wallaby was nibbling a slice of brown bread, watched enviously by a group of ducks. Two sealions were basking on the lake-side; the other was out of sight, probably relishing the shade and seclusion of the woodlands on the far bank.

Perhaps 'heavenly' was too strong a word, yet it seemed to fit. But even heaven is far from perfect; it takes a wild-life park manager to see the glaring idiosyncrasy which shatters the illusion of the Elysian Fields – the mythical abode of the blessed. They offer the idyllic existence for departed beings, human and animal, which includes hunters, predators, carnivores, herbivores, scavengers, parasites, microbes, and bacilli, which have all got to live, and whose several gratifications are mutually exclusive. Even immortality must be a fight for survival. What is more, no theological authority has ever divulged what precautions are taken in Paradise against outbreaks of anthrax, rabies, foot-and-mouth, pasteurella, or blight, which are, after all, only deserving micro-organisms trying to get a look-in. Only Red Indians, with their concept of a Happy Hunting Ground, allow for a compromise to eternity: theirs is an afterlife of work, sacrifice, violence, and natural selection. The other super-natural kingdoms are falsely advertised – Arcadia, Valhalla, Nirvana, Shangri La, Cricket St Thomas – you name it. If the celestial immortality is supposed to be the apotheosis of earthly mortality, then even up there, there is bound to be trouble from time to time.

Yet down here life had been surprisingly peaceful lately, John thought, as he surveyed the valley with satisfaction – no skirmishing, no sickness, no escapes, no bother. The animals were unusually quiet this morning – no howling dingoes, no screeching macaws, no hooting gibbons. Even the sealions were quiet. Yes, ominously quiet. Was this the calm before the storm? John walked across the dew-carpeted lawns back to the park office, contenting himself with the thought that at Cricket the riddle of the fox, the chicken, and the bag of corn had at last been solved. There was a letter waiting for him on his desk. The address was 'The Pampas', Tiverton. This would bring him back to reality perhaps.

Dear Sirs,
    I would like you to know how much we enjoyed your wild-life park. It is indeed a little bit of heaven. Surely Paradise could not be more beautiful,
                          yours faithfully,
                          E. K. Robinson (Mrs)

The doorbell rang – clamorous and persistent . . .